I0025500

AFOOT
IN THE DESERT

℞

A Contribution to Basic Survival

by
ALONZO W. POND, M.A.
Chief, Desert Branch
Arctic, Desert, Tropic Information Center

Fredonia Books
Amsterdam, The Netherlands

Afoot in the Desert:
A Contribution to Basic Survival

by
Alonzo W. Pond

ISBN: 1-4101-0889-9

Copyright © 2006 by Fredonia Books

Reprinted from the 1956 edition

Fredonia Books
Amsterdam, The Netherlands
http://www.fredoniabooks.com

All rights reserved, including the right to reproduce
this book, or portions thereof, in any form.

DESERT 4%

DESERT 20%

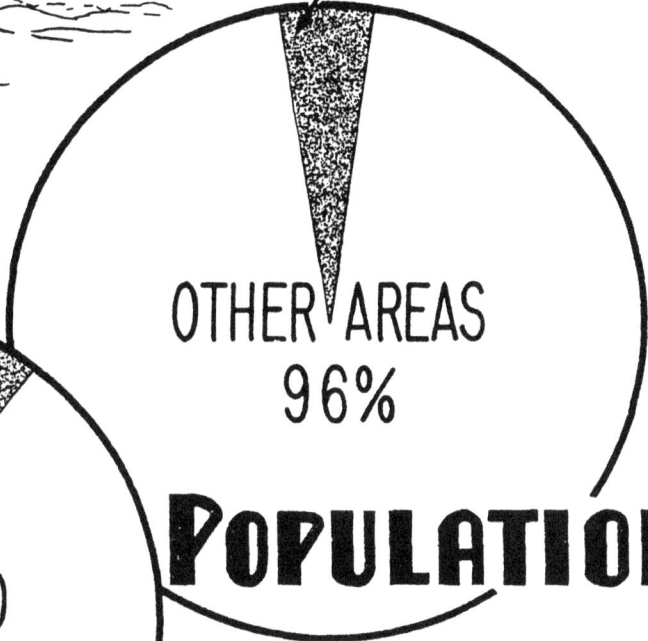

OTHER AREAS
96%

POPULATION

OTHER LAND
AREAS
80%

LAND AREA

Contents

Personal views or opinions expressed or implied in this publication are not to be construed as carrying official sanction of the Department of the Air Force or the Air University.

Introduction

"The man who knows HOW will always have a job, but the man who knows WHY will always be his boss," is an American proverb. Air Force Manual 64-5, "Survival," tells you the HOW with details. *Afoot in the Desert* tells you the WHY of desert survival. Read and use both.

Many of our long-held beliefs about living in desert climates have been made obsolete during the last few years. Recent scientific studies on water and heat exchanges in the human body make the old desert theories about thirst and ancient ideas on desert travel as out of date today as a Model T Ford or a World War I Jenny aircraft.

Afoot in the Desert is written to bring men in the Air Force up to date on desert living conditions. It is intended to provide basic information for escape and evasion in desert regions. It makes available the most recent, reliable information concerning survival needs of the human body in the deserts of the world.

There are numerous survival hints for you and me in the way desert plants and desert animals have adapted themselves to dry climate living. *Afoot in the Desert* shows you some of the lessons taught by plants and animals which have adjusted to life in dry climates. It gives you some idea of what to expect if you are forced down in these areas and find it necessary to live there until you can make it back to home and sweetheart.

Unfortunately the space available does not permit descriptions of the beauty, the fascination, and the charm of the world's great deserts. Neither does it allow for details about the interesting peoples who live in deserts. However, the information presented will make it easier for you to land, to live, and to travel afoot in the desert.

PART I

Typical Sahara landscape. These automobile tracks were made seven years before the photograph was taken. In that time there has not been enough sand blowing in this area to hide them. Note that there is not a spear of grass, a bush, or a tree—no sign of vegetation in this area.

DESERTS: WHAT AND WHERE THEY ARE

DESERTS are fascinating areas of majestic distances and extensive visibility. There is a military proverb that a man is not AWOL in the desert as long as he is in sight of camp, although it may take 3 days by jeep to reach him.

All desert areas are characterized by scanty rainfall and the absence of trees. Usually there is no open water in deserts but some deserts do have true lakes. Permanent desert lakes with no outlets are salt lakes. Fresh water pools may last days or weeks in any desert after unusual rainstorms. However, don't count on them when planning your desert promenade. It may be 15 or 20 years between those rainstorms.

Extremes of temperature are as characteristic of deserts as lack of rain and great distances. Hot days and cool nights are usual. A daily minimum-maximum range of 45°F in the Sahara and 25° to 35° difference between night and day in the Gobi is the rule. The difference between summer and winter temperatures is also extreme in deserts. Because of these extremes it is often difficult to keep from freezing in some desert areas. However, summer daytime heat in any desert of the world will make your sweat glands run at capacity production. You'll need drinking water to maintain that production.

There are more than 50 important[1] named deserts in the world. They occupy

[1] See Appendix 3.

1

Desert travelers crossing a sand dune in western Algeria. Only about 10% of the Sahara is sand dunes. Hundred-year-old maps of this area indicate the open spaces between the dunes and are accurate enough for present use.

Tamanrasset in the Hoggar Mountains of Central Sahara. In the Sahara, as in Southwest United States, mountains rise abruptly from the flat plain. This desert community was wiped out by flood a few years ago. Note the vegetation in this ancient river bed.

nearly one-fifth of the earth's land surface[2] but only about 4 percent of the world's population lives there.

Those areas dignified by the term "desert" vary greatly. There are salt deserts, rock deserts, and sand deserts. Some are barren gravel plains on which there is not a spear of grass, not a bush nor cactus spine for a hundred miles. In other deserts there are grass and thorny bushes where camels, goats, or even sheep can munch and nibble a subsistence diet.

In this study references are most often cited from two deserts of climatic extremes, a north temperate desert and a near tropic desert. Other deserts fall in between these extremes. Check your latitude when you compare these statements with your own particular desert.

Anywhere you find them, deserts are places of extremes. They are extremely dry, extremely hot, extremely cold, extremely free of plants or trees or lakes or rivers. But most important in any desert, it is an extremely long time between drinks unless you carry your water with you.

SAHARA

The Sahara is the largest desert in the world, as well as the best known. It stretches across North Africa from the Atlantic Ocean to the Red Sea; from the Mediterranean and the Sahara Atlas Mountains in the north to the Niger River in tropical Africa. Three million square miles of level plains and jagged mountains, rocky plateaus and graceful sand dunes! Thousands of barren miles where there is not a spear of grass, not a bush or tree, not a sign of vegetation! But Sahara oases, low spots in the desert where water can be reached for irrigation, are among the most densely populated areas in the world. Date groves and garden patches supporting 1,000 people per square mile are surrounded by barren plains devoid of life.

Only 10 percent of the Sahara is sandy. By far the greater part of the desert is flat gravel plain from which the sand has been blown away and piled up in the low places where the dunes are located. There are

rocky mountains rising 11 thousand feet above sea level, and there are a few depressions 50 to 100 feet below sea level.

The change from plain to mountain is abrupt in the Sahara. Mountains generally go straight up from the plain like jagged skyscrapers from a city street. Sharp-rising mountains on a level plain are especially noticeable in many desert landscapes because there is no vegetation to modify that abruptness. Because of the lack of trees or bushes even occasional foothills appear more abrupt than in temperate climates.

ARABIAN DESERT

Some geographers consider the Arabian Desert as a continuation of the Sahara. It covers most of the Arabian Peninsula except for fertile fringes along the Mediterranean, the Red Sea, the Arabian Sea and the valleys of the Tigris-Euphrates Rivers. Along much of the Arabian coast line the desert meets the sea.

There is more sand in the Arabian Desert than in the Sahara and there are fewer date grove oases. These are on the east side of the desert at Gatif, Hofuf, and Medina. Also there is some rain in Arabia each year in contrast to decades in Sahara without a drop. Accordingly Arabia has more widespread vegetation. Nomads find scanty pasture for their flocks of sheep and goats over large sections. They depend on wells for water. When unusual dry seasons threaten starvation to flocks these nomads move toward the fertile fringes of the desert. Historically the Arabian Desert has been the human reservoir from which people have pushed into more fertile regions. In drought years the border farmers still have to contend with nomad encroachment.

The Arabian Desert differs in one great respect from the Sahara. In Arabia there is oil. Aramco, or the Arabian American Oil Company, has established modern communities on the edge of the desert. They have drilled many water wells over the area for use of the nomads and their flocks.

Oil is carried across the desert in great pipelines which are regularly patrolled by planes. Pumping stations are located at intervals. All these evidences of modern civili-

---

[2]18 percent, according to Preston E. James, Geography of Man.

LOCATION of MAJOR Sand Deserts in AFRICA and ARABIA

Location of major sand deserts of Africa and Arabia.

zation have increased the well-being of the desert people and have increased your *chances* for a safe journey afoot. However, the desert of Arabia is rugged and native Arabs still get lost and die from dehydration.

GOBI

A few years ago, the Gobi, one of the great deserts of Central Asia, attracted popular attention because of the expeditions led by Dr. Roy Chapman Andrews and his discovery of dinosaur eggs. Today attention is again drawn to it because of its strategic location between China and the USSR. Some people use the term "Gobi" to cover all the desert regions between China and Russia. As used here, "Gobi" means that basin or saucer-like plateau north of China which includes Inner and Outer Mongolia.

On all sides of the Gobi there are mountains which form the rim of the basin. Many of them slope gently on the desert side but are abrupt and steep away from the basin. The basin itself slopes so gently that much of it appears like a level plain. There are rocks and buttes and numerous badlands or deeply gullied areas in the Gobi. The latter are the fossil hunting grounds which have given so many species of pre-historic animals to science. In spite of these obstacles, you can drive an automobile almost anywhere in the Gobi.

For a hundred miles or so around the rim of the desert there is a band of grassland. In average years the Chinese find this productive farm land. Year by year they push the Mongol herdsman farther and farther toward the true Gobi. In drought years agriculture retreats.

As you get deeper into the Gobi there is less and less rainfall; soil becomes thinner, and grass grows in scattered bunches. This is the home of the Mongol herdsman. His wealth is chiefly horses, but he also raises sheep and goats, camels, and a few cattle.

Beyond the rich grassland the Gobi floor is a mosaic of tiny pebbles which often glisten in the sunlight. These pebbles were once mixed with the sand and soil of the area, but in the course of centuries the soil has been washed or blown away and the pebbles left behind as a loose pavement.

What rain there is in the Gobi drains toward the basin; almost none of it cuts through the mountain rim to the ocean. There are some distinct and well-channeled watercourses, but these are usually dry. Many of them are remnants of prehistoric drainage systems. In the east numerous

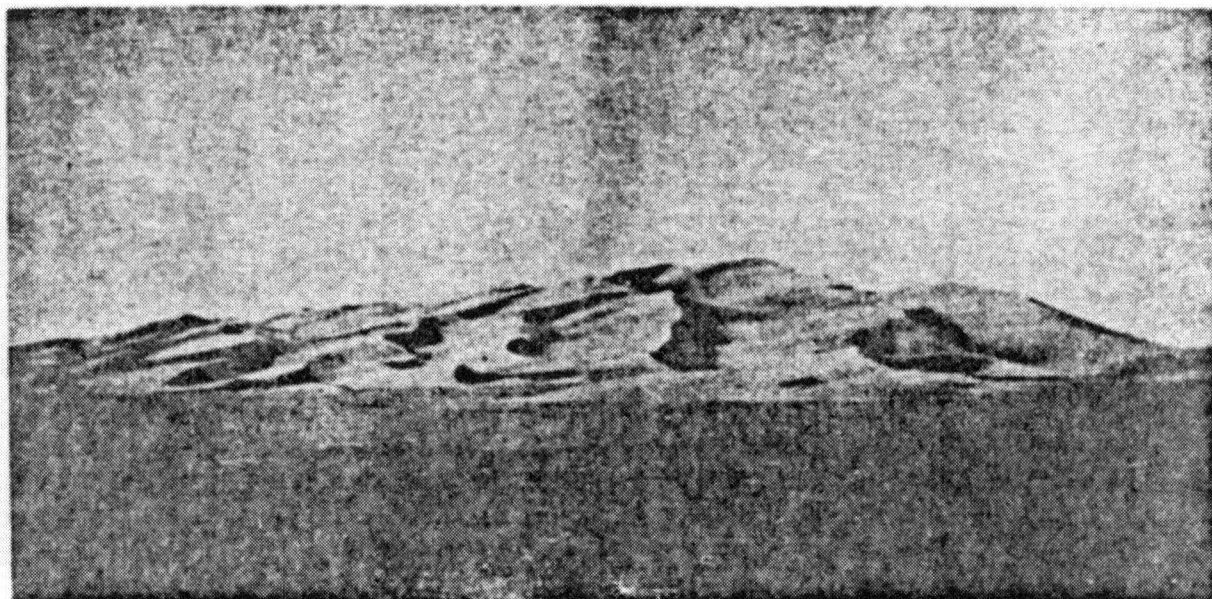

A Sahara sand dune. Note that the prevailing wind direction is from left to right.

shallow salt lakes are scattered over the plain. They vary in size and number with the changes in rainfall of the area.

Sand dunes are found in the eastern and western Gobi, but these are not as pronounced a feature of Mongolia as they are of certain sections in Sahara. The Gobi of Asia is not a starkly barren waste like the great African desert. Everywhere there is some grass, although it is often scanty. Mongols live in scattered camps all over the plains instead of being concentrated in oases.

SOUTHWEST UNITED STATES

The flat plains with scanty vegetation and abruptly rising buttes or mountains of our southwest are reminders both of the Gobi and of the Sahara. But the spectacular rock-walled canyons along the San Juan and Colorado Rivers (such as those around Rainbow Natural Bridge) have few counter-

parts in the deserts of Africa or Asia. The gullied badlands of the Gobi resemble similar formations in both southwest United States and the Dakotas, but our desert rivers, the lower Colorado, lower Rio Grande and tributaries, such as the Gila and Pecos, indicate a more regular supply of water than is found in Old World deserts. The Nile and Niger of course are in part desert rivers but get their water from tropical Africa. They are desert immigrant rivers (like the Colorado, which collects the melting snows of the eastern Rockies) and gain sufficient volume to carry them through the desert country.

The scattered population of Navajo, Apache, and Papago Indians who live in our southwest desert regions reminds one of the scattered population of Mongolia. In general our southwest deserts have more varied vegetation, greater variety of scenery, and a more rugged landscape than either

Typical camel pasture in the Gobi. In Mongolia the horizon is far distant. Grass is sometimes scanty and the desert surface paved with tiny pebbles. Camels are the principal beasts of burden in the Gobi and are raised for use on long caravan journeys from China to Central Asia.

Monument Valley, in southern Utah-northern Arizona. In the deserts of the Southwest United States there is more abundant vegetation than in most parts of the Gobi and Sahara. Note the abruptly rising buttes.

the Gobi or the Sahara. In all three areas it is often a long time between drinking water stops, and that makes a desert in any man's language.

Death Valley, a part of the Mohave lying between the Funeral Range and the Panamint Mountains, holds second place as the hottest desert, with an official maximum temperature of 134°F. The Sahara in Tripoli has an official high of 134.4°F to take first place. Actually, Death Valley probably has more water holes and more vegetation than exist in vast stretches of the Sahara. The evil reputation of the Valley appears to have been started by unwise travelers who were too terrified to make intelligent search for water and food. The dryness of Death Valley atmosphere is unquestioned, but it lacks the vast barren plains stretching from horizon to horizon which one finds in the Sahara. The sand dunes of Death Valley and nearby deserts make excellent movie stand-ins for Sahara dunes, but geographically they occupy far less territory than their African counterparts.

Compared to the Sahara the desert country of southwestern United States sometimes looks like a luxuriant garden. There are many kinds of cactus plants in the American desert, but these are not found in either the Gobi or Sahara.[3]

After a good spring rain—not every year by any means, but sometimes—there are more than 140 different kinds of plants which blossom in the American desert. Many of these are "quickies" whose seeds can withstand long months and even years of drought. White primroses, lavender verbenas, orange poppies, and yellow desert sunflowers are just a few of the colorful flowers which carpet the desert floor after a hard spring rain.

In contrast to the "quickies," which blossom only after desert rains, are the cactus plants. These store up moisture in their stems or trunks, and their blossom time is not so dependent on uncertain rains.

Although the cactus plants are not found in either the Gobi or the Sahara, both of these larger deserts do show a few of the quick-flowering species after a hard rain. The displays of flower colors in these Old World deserts, however, are very poor shows compared to the variety and brilliance of the American desert.

[3]As noted previously, the prickly pear has been imported to North Africa and grows abundantly in some oases on the northern edge of the Sahara; but it is not part of the wild desert vegetation except in America.

THE ADAPTATION OF LIFE IN THE DESERT—THE LESSON FROM NATURAL OR BIOLOGICAL ADAPTION

A Mehari or desert-riding camel in typical Sahara pasture. His food storage is the hump on his back, and his water storage is extra tanks in his belly.

PLANTS, animals, and human beings live under desert conditions. All three have found ways to survive under extremes of heat and scarcity of water. Certain plants have been more successful in adjusting to the desert than other forms of life. Some animals have adopted more successfully than man. In all cases the adaptation to desert conditions is primarily an adjustment to long, very long, periods without water.

PLANTS

Desert plants have several characteristics which enable them to make use of available water and to resist long periods of drought. Some plants have extensive root systems which cover large areas to take advantage of surface moisture from desert rains. Other plants have roots which penetrate to considerable depths. Travelers who find a tiny dead stick on the desert plain pull or dig out its root system to obtain enough fuel to boil their tea, although the uninitiated would not expect that a finger-thick, 2-inch stub could be a supply of fire wood.

In addition to extensive root systems, these desert plants develop rosettes of leaves which hug the ground closely for protec-tion against wind and excessive loss of water. Many plants develop tiny spine-like leaves which resist evaporation while carrying on their job of making food for the plant.

The cactus plants found in American deserts have thick stems instead of leaves in which the green chlorophyl carries on the food-producing work. These thick stems also store moisture needed by the plant.

One of the most interesting adaptations is the ability of some plants to produce drought-resistant seeds. When a desert rain does occur, these seeds sprout quickly, grow rapidly, flower, and produce a new crop of seeds. They survive in the desert by avoiding desert dryness and "living" only when water is avaliable. The speed and energy with which these colorful members of the mustard family can take advantage of a sudden rain is startling. For years a patch of the Sahara may be as bare and dry as a concrete pavement. A few days after a hard rain, the desert becomes a beautiful flowered carpet of vegetation. Camels led into such unusual pasture make a fantastic picture. The ungainly beasts wander about with pretty purple blossoms dangling from their ugly faces.

In dry river beds, shallow basins, and hollows between sand dunes, scattered bunches of coarse grass and shrubs are found. This vegetation is so sparse that camels have a leisurely walk between bites when turned into these pastures.

Actually, desert vegetation varies from non-existent in some parts of Sahara to good grass pasture in the Gobi where horses are raised in large herds. The presence or absence of plants depends on the quantity and frequency of moisture. Sometimes that moisture is ground water which roots can reach even when no rain falls. Elsewhere vegetation depends entirely on rain. In oases regular crops are raised by irrigation from wells, tunnels, or diverted surface streams.

Photo by Carleton S. Coon.

Typical desert vegetation in the Khorasan of Iran. Dried stalks of annual plants
like this are excellent for a quick, hot fire.

ANIMALS

A few animals have been able to adjust their body processes to desert conditions. The best known of these, of course, are the camel and the gazelle. Apparently the desert antelope or gazelle is able to get enough moisture for its needs from the grasses or other vegetation it eats. There are no records

Adult gazelle from Algerian Sahara. Various species of these swift animals are found in most deserts. Hunters and scanty vegetation in Sahara and Arabia keep down the population of gazelles. In the Central Gobi of Mongolia large bands of such animals are common. In late summer herds sometimes include many thousands of females and young while the bucks keep to themselves.

to indicate that these pretty creatures ever drink water. In both Sahara and the Gobi they live where there is no open water. They do have to eat, however, so you will not find them where all vegetation is lacking.

Camels on the other hand, have adapted to an irregular supply of water, not to its absence. In Sahara native herdsmen start training camels when they are calves to take water at intervals of about 4 days. Then, when they are full grown, they can go 6 or 8 days without a drink. There are records of camels going 10 days without water even when working in summer heat. But whatever the period of drought a camel undergoes, it must make up for in the end.

How long the camel goes without drink-

ing depends on his surroundings. In winter temperatures when the pasturage contains some moisture, his water needs are low. Under ideal pasture conditions in the winter camels have been known to go 4 months or longer without drinking. However, camel men say that their charges drink about as much water per year as other beasts of equal size. They may drink as much as 6 gallons per day on hot days.

Until recently it was believed that camels stored water in the linings of their multiple stomachs. In 1954 Dr. Knut Schmidt-Nielson carefully studied the camel's drinking habits in the Sahara. He also dissected several specimens. He found that camels do not store water. Instead they have adapted to desert conditions by a wide body temperature range, by the rigid conservation of body moisture, and by their tolerance of a very high percentage of dehydration.

A healthy man's body temperature varies less than 2°F. The camel's daily range is 12.6°F, more than six times as great! The camel's body temperature may be down to 93.2°F in the morning, and reach 105.8°F in the heat of the day. With that range, he doesn't need to start sweating as soon as other animals.

The camel's woolly coat helps conserve his sweat by keeping the hot desert air away from his body and by letting his sweat evaporate most efficiently. Another important water-saving adaptation the camel has which man lacks is his ability to eliminate body wastes in a highly concentrated urine. When the camel must sweat he can dehydrate up to 30 percent of his body weight, several times man's safe dehydration limit. In short, the camel uses his water more efficiently, and can go deeper into water-debt than man.

After a period of dehydration the camel drinks enough water to pay off the debt or replace that used by his body since the last drink. The water he drinks is absorbed quickly so that his body fluids and tissues are brought back to normal water content in a few hours. He drinks only enough to restore his body's weight, and stores absolutely no surplus against future needs.

The green, odorous liquid in the camel's stomachs, which some desert travelers have used as a last resort, is composed of partly digested vegetation and digestive juices. It contains moisture and nourishment for the man who can stomach the stuff, but it is not excess or stored water. Nevertheless it may help prolong your life a little.

Dr. Schmidt-Nielson's discoveries have not changed the fact that camels can go long periods without water. His work does show that the animals withstand dryness by a greater tolerance of heat and dehydration instead of by a water storage system. Deprived of water beyond the limits of his dehydration range, the camel dies of "thirst" (actually dehydration) just as man does when dehydrated beyond his limits of tolerance.

Although the camel does not carry excess water, he has an advantage in the matter of food. The hump is all fat, and a food reserve, built up firm and solid during months in good pasture. When out on desert trails where food is scarce, the hump is gradually absorbed to supply the energy that keeps the animal going. A soft or flabby hump is an application for 6 months annual leave. Wise owners grant that leave—or lose their camels.

The use of the energy stored in the hump requires less water for waste elimination than energy obtained from eating forage. When the body converts the hump fat into energy, it produces a small amount of waste and some water. This water helps carry away the waste and delays dehydration. The hump is another of the camel's physical adaptations to living in dry regions.

The camel moves in slow motion to generate as little body heat as possible, and his coat insulates his body against excess heat from the desert air. Man can move slowly, keep sheltered from desert heat by seeking shade, and insulate his body with clothing. His greater need for water compared to that of the camel, however, makes it necessary for man to carry all his water with him.

Like the camel, but within narrower limits, man can restore his body weight quickly after a period of dehydration by drinking large quantities of water.

Some rodents and other small animals have also learned to live in deserts. These conserve their moisture by keeping in shade or burrowing underground. They thus shield themselves from the direct sun and avoid heated air and the hot surface of the desert. They have digestive systems that enable them to manufacture all the water they need from the starches they eat. They expend very little moisture in eliminating their body wastes. Their feces are very dry, and their urine much more concentrated than in man or other animals not adapted to living under drought conditions.

Man does develop more sweat glands per square inch of skin surface if he is raised in the desert or hot climates from infancy. That adaptation makes it easier for him to live in the heat, but *it does not lessen his need for water.*

Man gets along in the desert by carrying his supply of food and water with him. So far we know of no desert men with flesh and blood storage humps. Man's food hump is either a pack on his back or a pack on the back of his transportation, whether that be beast or vehicle. He may carry a quart of water in his belly, enough for a 5-mile hike, but, like his food, most of his water supply is in auxiliary tanks of some sort. Intelligent desert travelers keep to trails where wells are located. They take advice from desert rats and keep out of the heat as much as possible. They adopt the philosophy of the camel, which is strictly slow motion.

Oasis dwellers, of course, are not true desert men. Food and water are present in the oasis just as they are on farms in temperate areas. Oasis people do hunt shelter during the heat of desert summers, and they take life slow and easy, like wise tropic dwellers. In winter they hunt the sunny side of a nice warm wall.

PART III

The Colorado River, an immigrant desert stream that cuts through the barren rock plateau of northern Arizona.

MAN'S ADAPTATION—THE APPLICATION OF NATURE'S LESSON

DESERT WATER

MOTHER EARTH, Father Sky, Brother Wind, Friend Light, Sweetheart Water. . ." says an Indian song. An Arab proverb adds: "Three things there are that ease the heart from sorrow: water, green grass, and the beauty of women."

Major General Collins, commenting on the Libyan Campaign, 1941, put the matter more bluntly when he said, "Water has been and may be again the crux of the whole show."

Poet, philosopher, and general agree on the importance of water, for the one great truth about the desert is: Where there is water there is life.

Desert oases are proof of that statement. As water becomes available through new wells or irrigating projects, date groves and garden patches spread into once barren desert. When the wells go dry, the desert reclaims the area.

In all deserts, wells are the sources of most water. Hand-dug wells have furnished water to irrigate Sahara oases for many centuries, and there are almost as many ways of hauling the water to the surface as there are wells. Hand-dug wells, like the oases themselves, are located in low places of the desert. Basins, dry river valleys, and hollows in the dunes are typical locations. The best of these, of course, are ancient river beds.

In western Sahara the natives have dug elaborate tunnels for irrigation. Starting at the edge of a basin or in the bed of an old river, they dig a ditch toward the desert, keeping the bottom of the ditch on a gentle slope away from the basin. As the ditch extends out into the desert it soon becomes too deep to be maintained as an open trench. The workmen extend it as a tunnel as far as they can see without artificial light. Leapfrogging ahead along the same line,

12

An oasis in the Sahara. The Arabs say that palm trees must have their feet in the water and their heads in eternal sunshine.

they set down a well and tunnel back and forward. Then another jump is made and another well. Eventually these chains of wells, connected by a tunnel in the moist sand, extend for miles into the desert. Water collects in the underground channel and flows to the basin, where it irrigates the gardens. These systems are called *foggaras* in Sahara, *khotteras* in Morocco, *qanats* in Iraq and Iran, *karez* or *kariz* in Iran, Iraq, Afghanistan, and central Asia, *feledj* in southern Arabia. Lines of such wells are often visible from the air. They mean water and will lead you to desert communities.

The Gobi is itself a great basin with only internal drainage so that water falling on its mountain edges, if not evaporated, replenishes the ground water supply. Wells dug in valley bottoms or other low places of the Gobi tap that water supply at 10 to

15 feet depth. Natives dip the water with a skin bag on the end of a stick to which a rope is attached or use a bucket on a hand rope. Elaborate pulleys, well sweeps, or pumps so common in the Sahara are not necessary at shallow Gobi wells.

In northern Mongolia, wells are less numerous than in the south because there are more springs. All roads lead to water, however. You'll know you are going in the right direction when your trail joins another. The "arrow" formed by two connecting trails points toward the water.

Great desert rivers like the Nile, the Tigris, and the Euphrates have been used to irrigate the desert for centuries. Shorter streams on the desert edges are also diverted into irrigation ditches to water the feet of palm trees. At other points where mountain streams lose themselves in desert sands the natives plant their trees and crops right over the lost rivers so that roots can reach the water without difficulty.

There are shallow lakes in most deserts, and many of them are undrained. These have been without outlets for many thousands of years so that evaporation has concentrated the amount of salt in the water and has made them distinctly salt water lakes. Some of the salt water tastes like table salt. In other areas it may contain magnesium or alkali. If not too strong, such waters are drinkable even though they may have a laxative effect. Alkali wells in the Gobi may make you prefer to go 6 or 8 miles farther for fresher water.

Bad-tasting water, often the source of stories about poisoned wells, may not be seriously harmful. Only two wells in Sahara, both in Esh-Shesh Erg, are poisonous. One is so rich in chlorine it will burn clothing; the other has so much saltpeter the water causes vomiting. In southwestern United States some desert springs contain arsenic salts. You can recognize these by the absence of vegetation, always abundant around good springs, and usually by the nearby remains of wild and domestic animals killed by drinking the poisonous water.

In the Sahara deep hollows on rocky plains act as cisterns and collect surface water from the rare torrential rains. These

Desert nomad's tent on the edge of sand dunes. The wool tent is close to the ground and the walls are easily lifted to provide ventilation during the heat of the day, or lowered in the cool of the night.

The water hole at Tigelmimi, a day's auto run South of InSalah, Algerian Sahara Desert. This is really a natural cistern which receives the drainage from the surrounding desert rock when rare desert rains occur in the area. When the photo was taken the pool was deep enough (4 feet) for a swimming hole.

tanks may be dry for 10 or 15 years, then suddenly be deep enough for a good swimming hole. The water in them is fresh and drinkable and may take several weeks or months to dry up. Unfortunately there is no way for the casual traveler or stranger to the area to know of the existence of such water holes, and there is no rule to guide one to them. They are natural drainage basins like any depression on a plain or plateau. If you know there has been a rain recently in your area, then keep an eye out for hollows or any protected cavity which would naturally collect surface drainage.

The thirsty traveler in tropical jungles will find many plants containing suitable drinking water. In the Gobi and Sahara, plants are not a source of water supply. American deserts are slightly better favored. The large barrel cactus does contain considerable moisture which can be squeezed

Typical Mongol camp on the Gobi plateau, including felt yurts and cotton tents. Some horses are always tied to a picket line, as Mongols object to walking even a few feet. Note that the walls of some of the yurts have been raised to permit circulation of air.

out of the pulp if you have the energy to cut through the tough, outer spine-studded rind. Botanists argue that the juice *can be used* and *cannot be used* to quench thirsts. Randall Henderson and his two companions did drink it. They found the taste bitter. "Reminded me of the taste when I take an aspirin tablet without a drink of water to wash it down," says Henderson. The taste disappeared in about half an hour. A barrel cactus 3½ feet high contained moisture from top to bottom and "about a quart of liquid could be obtained by crude methods of crushing the pulp and squeezing out the milky juice." (This is an exception, like dandelions, to the rule that milky or colored sap-bearing plants should not be eaten.) Working with a scout knife, Henderson once took 40 minutes to get to the moisture-bearing pulp of this kind of plant. Less time was required when a machete was available[5]. So far the evidence for getting

your water supply out of desert plants indicates that you had better find a well.

Desert wells are generally located along trails. In rocky deserts and on some gravel plains, however, it is not always easy to find the well. This is particularly true if it does not have any super structure or is in a protected valley.

In desert and near-desert regions, wells are gathering places for native peoples as well as stopping places for caravans. Permanent camps or habitations may be some distance away from the well, sometimes as much as 2 or 3 miles away. Passing caravans may camp within a few yards or a few hundred yards from a well. Camp fire ashes, animal droppings, and generally disturbed surface will tell you that others have camped there. Such indications will also tell you that a well is not far off. Paths leading from the camping area should lead you to the well.

Many desert water holes are not true wells but are natural tanks or cisterns. These may be located behind rocks, in gullies or side canyons and under cliff edges. Often the ground surface near them is solid rock or hard-packed soil on which paths do not

[5] In 1942 Edwin Waldislaus Zolnier, 1st. Lieutenant, USMCR parachuted from his burning plane out in Arizona and roamed the desert for 5 days. He tried the juice of several cacti which were "very nauseating" before he discovered the barrel type. He "gouged large chunks out of the living cactus and chewed the water content out of it." The juice completely satisfied his thirst and the taste was pleasant at first but became monotonous after a few days. Chunks of the cactus were carried for several days and still had moisture in them. The marine also rubbed his body with the pieces he had chewed. This moisture helped keep him cool. (From his letter July 31, 1944, quoted by Ladislaus Cutak in Missouri Botanical Garden Bulletin.)

show up. In such cases you may have to search for the water point. In the Libyan Sahara, doughnut-shaped mounds of camel dung often surround the wells. Unless you recognize the small mound ring you could easily miss the well.

On some flat plains, wells which are not often used are covered against sandstorms. Even though there is no sand in the immediate area, sandstorms would in time fill up such wells. In sand dune areas this is even more likely. Desert people have learned to cover such wells a little below the top. Sand drifts in, but the well is protected. You can dig out the cover and reach water easily in such wells but be careful and don't dump the sand into the cavity. There may be only a shallow pool of water in the well bottom.

When you are away from trails or far from wells, you may still find water. Along the seashore or on sandy beaches or desert lakes your best chance is to dig a hole in the first depression behind the first sand dune. Rain water from local showers collects here. Stop digging when you hit wet sand. Water will seep out of the sand into the hole. This first water is fresh or nearly fresh. It is drinkable. If you dig deeper, you may strike salt water.

Damp surface sand anywhere marks a good place to scoop out such a shallow "well," from which you can collect water into your canteen or other receptacle. Among sand dunes away from surface water the lowest point between the dunes is where rain water will collect. Dig down 3 to 6 feet. If sand gets damp, keep digging until you hit water. If you dig in the dune itself you may strike a foot or so of damp sand with dry sand below. When that happens, you had better look for a lower spot to dig your well.

In a sand dune belt, water will most likely be found beneath the original valley floor at the edge of the dunes rather than in the easy digging middle.

You may find water in sand dune areas if you dig in the hollow near the steep side of the dune.

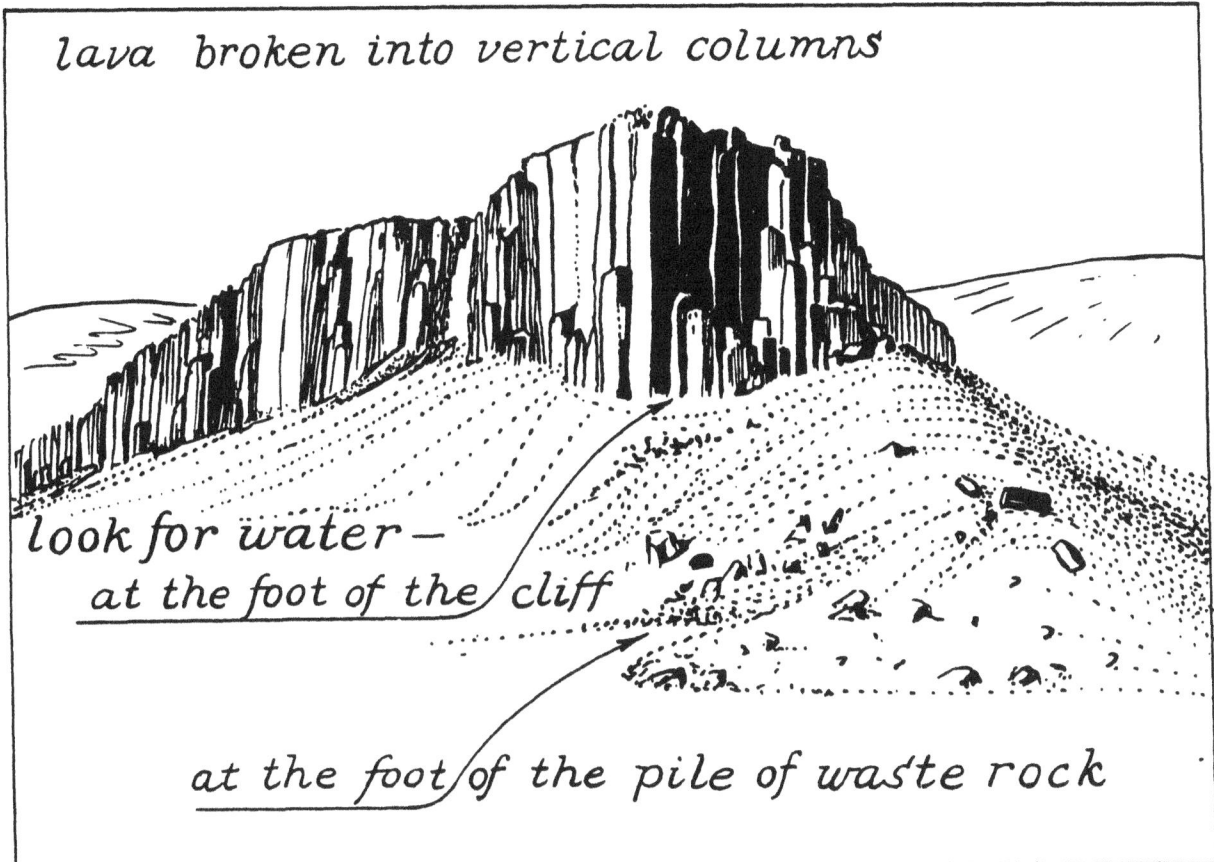

lava broken into vertical columns

*look for water —
at the foot of the cliff*

at the foot of the pile of waste rock

Water may be found at the base of rock cliffs for some weeks or months after a desert rain. It is also found in the waste rock at the base of cliffs or in the gravel outwash from valleys in mountains which may get regular seasonal rain or snow. This is particularly true of mountains on the edge of deserts.

Dry stream beds often have water just below the surface. It accumulates and sinks at the lowest point on the outside of a bend in the stream channel as the stream dries up. You may catch a drink if you dig on such outside bends.

In mud flats during winter you may find wet mud at the lowest point. Wring mud out in a piece of cloth to get water—but don't drink if the water is too salty or soapy tasting.

In the Arabian Desert near the Persian Gulf and the Red Sea and in the Libyan Sahara near the Mediterranean Sea there is considerable moisture in the air. This moisture will condense on cool objects. Often condensed moisture or dew will be heavy enough to drip from metal awnings or roofs on cool mornings. In Arabia this morning dew and even fog extends inland several

miles. Occasionally fog occurs as much as 200 miles from the Persian Gulf.

In the Negev, desert of Israel, ancient piles of stone are found in regular lines. In some of them old stumps of grape vines have been discovered. Some archaeologists believe that the ancients heaped stones around the grape vine base so that dew would collect and water the vines.

If you find dew on the metal wings of your crashed plane you may collect the drip in a container or you might get more water by wiping it off the cool metal with a handkerchief or soft cloth and wringing it out into a container.

Cool stones, collected from below the hot surface of the desert, if placed on a waterproof tarp may cause enough dew to collect for a refreshing drink. Exposed metal surfaces like airplane wings or tin cans

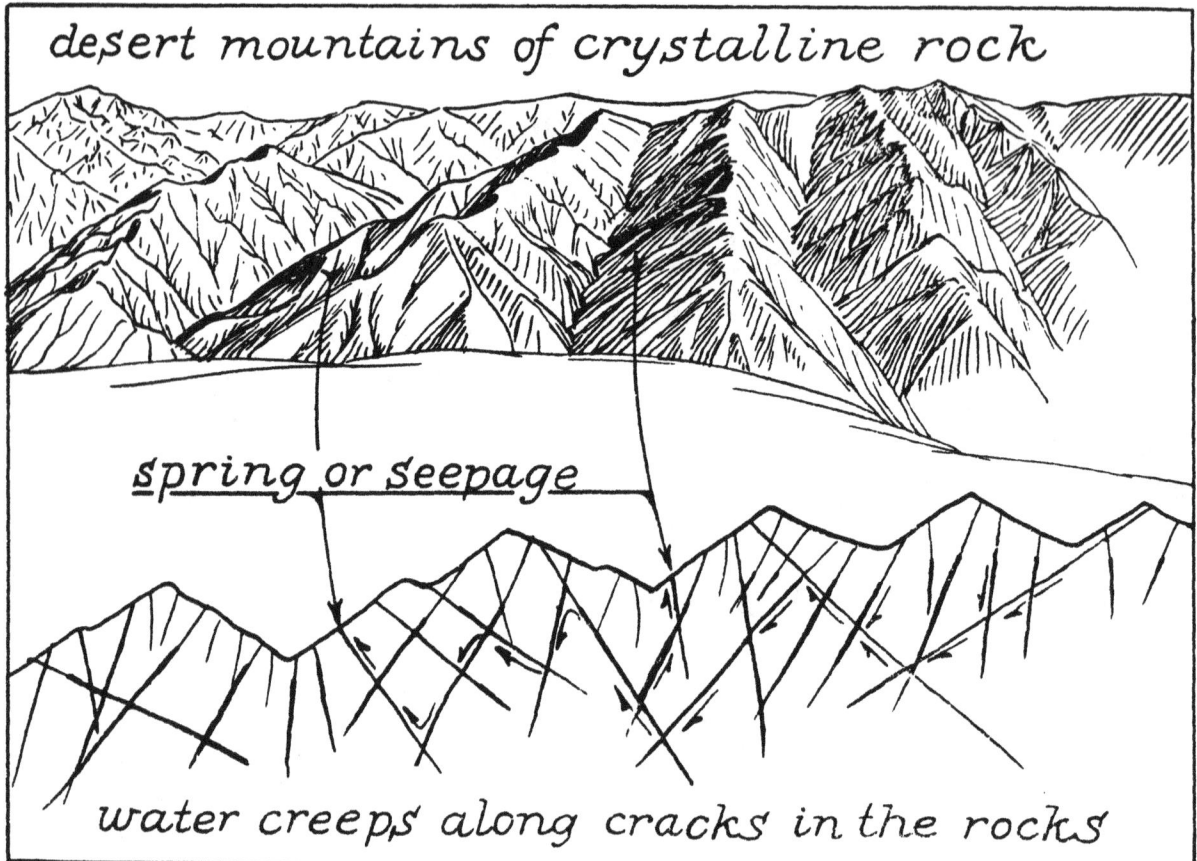

desert mountains of crystalline rock

spring or seepage

water creeps along cracks in the rocks

Where to look for springs in hard rock mountains of the desert.

are best dew condensers. They should be clean of dust or grease to get the best flavored water.

Soon after sunrise in the desert the dew evaporates. If you expect a good drink you will have to collect the dewdrops very soon after sunup.

Desert natives often know of lingering surface pools in dry stream beds or other low places. They cover them in various ways to protect them from excessive evaporation. If you look under likely brush heaps or in sheltered nooks you may locate such pools in semiarid brush country.

Birds all need water. Some of them fly considerable distances at sunset and dawn to reach water holes. If you hear their chirping in the early morning or evening you may locate their private drinking fountain. In true desert areas flocks of birds will circle over water holes.

The presence of vegetation does not al-ways mean that surface water is available. Many desert plants have extensive shallow root systems for gathering the maximum moisture from desert showers. Others, euca-lyptus for instance, have taproots that go down to ground water. Suez canal diggers found tamarisk roots 100 feet down. In American deserts mesquite is an excellent water-indicating plant. Though sometimes so buried by drifting sand that only 2 or 3 feet of brownish tips protrude, where mesquite grows you can reach water, if you dig—but it may be down 30 to 60 feet!

Damp places where flies hover are better spots to dig. Surface water was there re-cently. Donkeys and goats gone wild often make trails to dry riverbeds. These some-times lead to little meadows of short reeds almost hidden under a few bushes, where the animals paw holes in the spongy ground. At such spots you may get drinking water 2 or 3 feet below the surface.

DESERT FOOD

Food, like water, in the true deserts must be carried with you. When you reach an oasis you are no longer in the desert in the survival sense, for you have reached a populated area. Food is less important than water. You can get along without food for several days with no ill effects.

There are numerous stories about poisonous plants in the desert, and natives, especially in the Sahara, have a notion that most plants are poisonous. Grasses, of course, are edible, but the few plants one will find in the Sahara or the Gobi are not likely to be either palatable or nutritious. The general rule is to avoid plants with milky or colored sap, but it is safe to taste anything. If you don't like it, spit it out. A taste won't kill you even if it is pioson. (See Appendix 4.)

Animal food will be difficult to find in the Sahara. Gazelles do exist but are kept well hunted out by the desert soldiers. In the Gobi the story is entirely different. Antelopes are numerous in many parts of the Gobi. It is not uncommon to see herds of ten to a hundred animals. You may also strike areas where there are none at all.

Wolves are found in rugged terrain near good antelope pasture. Around occasional springs or water holes in old river beds many birds are found night and morning. In spring and fall, ducks and other waterfowl are numerous. In fact, game is generally available in the Gobi, but so are domestic animals.

The natives of Mongolia live in scattered family units, like the Navajo Indians in southwestern United States, instead of in villages like argricultural people. They raise sheep and goats, horses, camels, and cattle. They also keep large, unfriendly dogs. Flocks and herds are guarded and are taken to water twice a day. In an emergency it is better to appeal to the natural hospitality of the native than to risk his anger by destroying his property.

Once natives have been contacted in any desert, food and water are available. In normal times desert people are hospitable. Native food in the Sahara is both palatable and edible. The meat offered you may be goat or mutton or chicken. In rare cases it may be camel. Steamed wheat flour pellets, which look like a great platter of rice, is *cous-cous* and really good eating. The vegetables which go with it you will recognize.

The food available in the Gobi, you will also recognize. Natives eat cheese and butter and buttered tea, also some rice. In recent years under Russian tutelage they have been urged to eat bread and vegetables. You are less likely to enjoy native food in the Gobi than in the Sahara, as many Mongols have less idea of cleanliness and sanitation than the Arabs and the Berbers.

HEALTH AND HAZARDS

Deserts are quite healthy places. Dry air is not favorable to bacteria.[7] Wounds usually heal rapidly in the desert, even without treatment. Except in some oases of the Sahara, malaria does not exist. The social diseases, however, are prevalent in both Gobi and Sahara. They are much more common in Mongolia than in Africa. Until you lose your sense of sight and your sense of smell, you will probably not become contaminated.

Since Russian domination of Outer Mongolia it is reported that scientific treatment of social diseases has reduced their prevalence considerably.

Contagious diseases are generally not as common in the Gobi and Mongolia as they are in densely populated China. However, several diseases are reported from Chahar on the southern border of Mongolia. Among these is trachoma, so keep your eyes clean.

Summertime dysentery can be avoided by watching your diet and not eating or drinking uncooked native food. In the fall and early winter, typhoid and paratyphoid are present, but your inoculation shots will give you normal protection from these.

Crowded living quarters in family *yurts* or in adobe lamaseries and inadequate diet during winter and early spring are probably responsible for the appearance of tubercu-

[7] Under wartime conditions with thousands of men in limited areas without proper sanitation facilities, dysentary and other diseases were common. Afoot in the Desert is concerned with survival conditions away from crowds.

Tuareg woman and Negro woman from the Hoggar of Sahara. The Tuaregs are white people whose skin color is about the same shade as that of Italians. The Negroes of the Hoggar have come from Central Africa. Although they are Mohammedans, Tuareg women do not veil their faces.

losis and the seasonal occurrence of scurvy among some natives. The Mongols believe that scurvy can be cured by drinking lots of milk. Proper diet, of course, is your protection against contracting either scurvy or tuberculosis.

Any American who follows his natural habits of cleanliness and his normal ideas of diet will find the deserts of the world quite free from disease, probably safer in that respect than the crowded cities of the United States or Europe.

Ordinarily mosquitoes do not travel far from their breeding place. They breed in quiet or stagnant water such as rain pools, swamps, water pockets in plants, old tin cans or similar places. Since their usual life span is 15 to 20 days, under some conditions even a couple of months, their presence does not mean that you are near a supply of water. In 1942 sentries in the Libyan Sahara saw "a cloud of vapour

coming from the north which looked like a duststorm by moonlight." The "cloud" was a swarm of mosquitoes, and the nearest breeding places were 18 to 28 miles to the northeast. A strong wind carried the insects into the desert. Possibly they could have traveled even farther.[8]

All mosquitoes are unwelcome company but only some species of the genus Anopheles carry malaria. You can usually distinguish Anopheles from other mosquitoes by the way they settle on your skin or other surface. Anopheles settles with the pro-

Tuareg men from the Hoggar of Sahara. The men of this tribe hide their faces with veils. Note that like all desert people their skin is well protected from sun, wind, and cold, although the garments are loose. Sandals are the only footgear worn in this area.

---

[8]Salt marsh mosquitoes will migrate 30-40 miles. Some wind carried insects reach even greater distances.

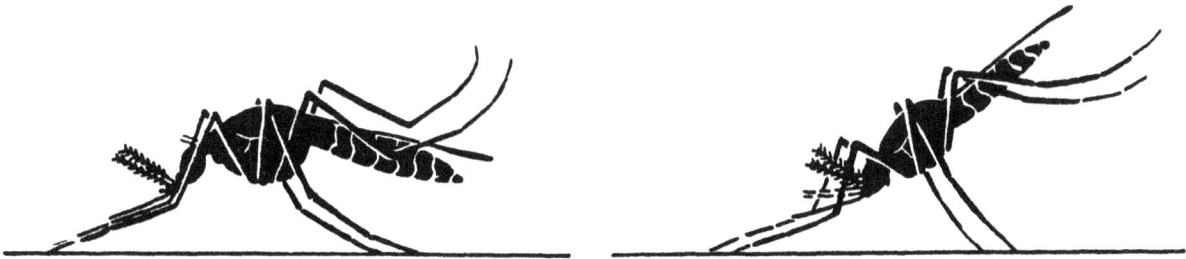

Mosquitoes
Left—**This gal can sing and bite but rarely carries disease.** She is a Culicine female and perches nearly parallel to her landing field. Right—**Anopheles lands at about a 45° angle and makes no noise.** If she has recently had a meal of malaria infected blood, she can communicate the disease to you.

boscis and long axis of the body in one straight line (see fig. 22) at an angle of 45° with its "landing field." The Culicine mosquitoes, which in general do not carry disease, land with the abdomen parallel to or inclined toward the surface upon which it rests. Cold weather slows them up.[9]

Singing mosquitoes are not Anopheles. The singers do not generally carry disease. Malaria, yellow fever, dengue, filariasis (elephantiasis) and other ills are mosquito borne.

Unless the female Anopheles has bitten a patient with malaria or other mosquito-carried disease before she bites you, no harm is done. She is only a vector, not an originator. If a strong silent mosquito drills you at a 45° angle play safe and reach for the Chloroquin.[10]

Flies are sometimes found so far out in the desert that you wonder how they got there. In Egypt and Libya they are *bad*. They buzz and pry about any exposed part of your body with persistent malignity. They settle on your lips, the corners of your eyes, your ears. There is no rest from flies unless you cover your face and every part of your body when you are in a fly-infested desert.

Since WW II, many areas have been treated against flies. If garbage is covered, kitchens, food-handling areas, and sleeping quarters are screened, relief from flies is possible. If you travel in the desert they will probably be hitchhiking on your back, but in time you can get rid of them until you reach another inhabited area.

Other insects are less numerous. In some regions you might shake a scorpion out of your shoes in the morning. On the other hand you can spend months in the desert without seeing one.

In Arabia the nomad women keep down the lice population by washing their hair every week in camel urine. It is strong stuff which is tough on the current generation of bugs but a new generation follows before the week is out.

Snakes are not numerous in desert areas. Some individuals manage to see snakes where others, just as sober, see none at all. An American scientific expedition in the Gobi of Mongolia once camped on the private property of a nest of vipers. Every man in the outfit was killing snakes for an hour or two, but other years the same group saw almost no live snakes. Cold weather keeps them sluggish, and you probably will not see one in wintertime even in southern deserts.

A really *serious hazard* exists in the WW II fought-over regions of Libyan Sahara. These are the mine fields which have not been cleared except for limited roads. The engineers who were assigned the clean-up job lost so many men that only necessary routes through the fields were cleared. The attached map gives some still dangerous general areas. In these localities you should seek special local advice and "tread lightly."[11]

[9]Mosquitoes in arctic or sub-arctic regions will bite at much lower temperatures.

[10]Recent discoveries indicate that mosquitoes of the genus Haemagogus and Aedes, which breed in rock pools and treetops, serve as vectors for yellow fever. Several species of Aedes also carry dengue fever. Certain species of all main groups of mosquitoes can transmit filariasis. Culex and Aedes transmit encephalitis. Psorophora carries dermatobia.

[11]See Appendix 2, List of Mine Hazards in Libya.

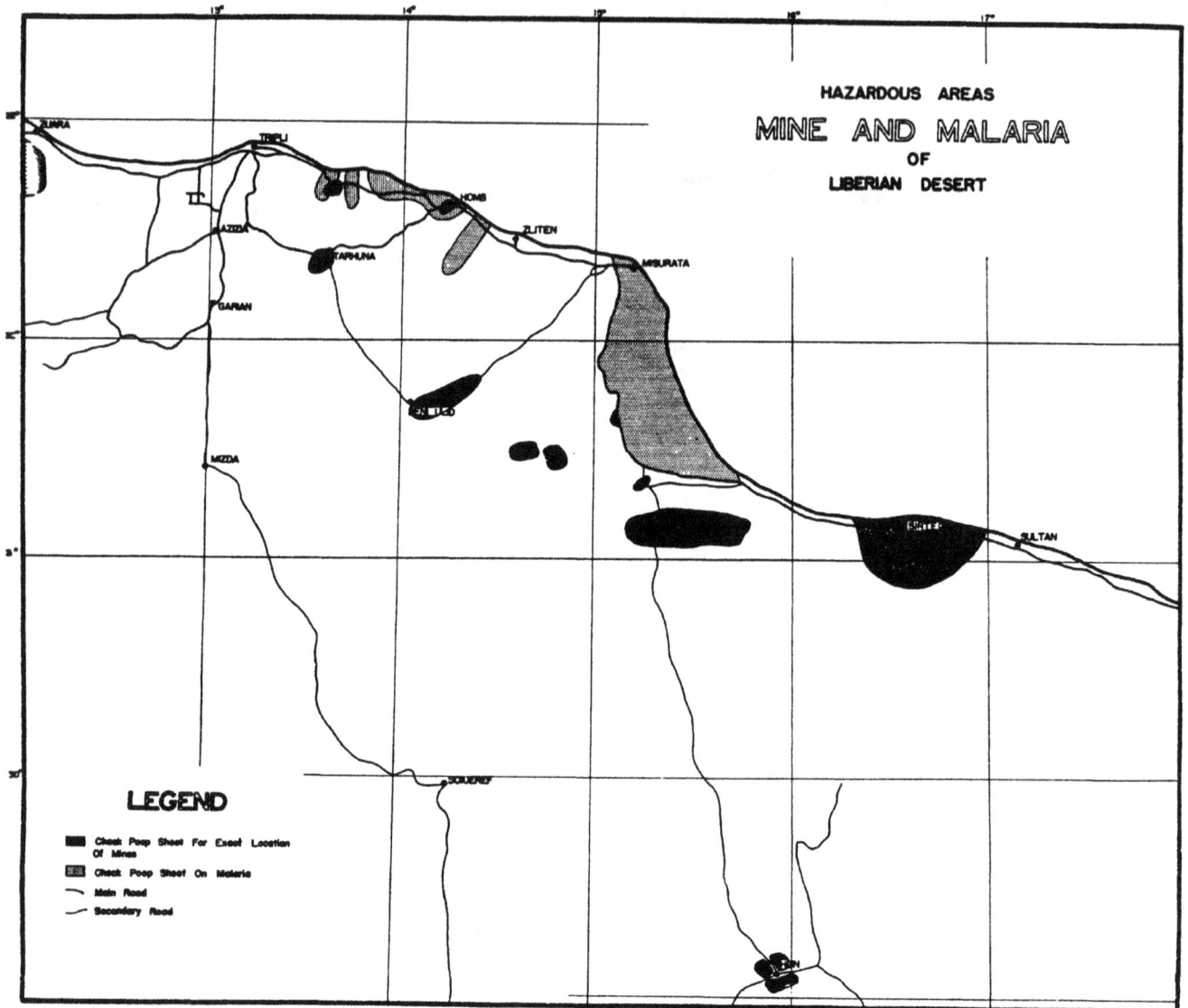

HAZARDOUS AREAS
MINE AND MALARIA
OF
LIBERIAN DESERT

LEGEND
▓ Check Poop Sheet For Exact Location Of Mines
▒ Check Poop Sheet On Malaria
— Main Road
— Secondary Road

Location of Malaria and Mine Hazards.

Sandstorms are not a serious hazard unless you make them so. If you try to travel when visibility is zero you can get lost in a hurry. That is true on a black desert night when sentries can't find their post or miss a white tent at 50 feet. It is true in severe sand or dust storms.

If wind and dust impede your progress or shut out visibility, stop traveling! Mark the direction you are traveling with a deep scratched arrow on the ground, a row of stones or other markers. Then lie down and sleep out the storm with your back to the wind. You may get some comfort by covering your face with cloth.

Don't worry about being buried by a sandstorm. Desert romance stories have got to make the storms good, but no man was ever buried alive by a desert sandstorm. Even in the sand dune areas it takes years for the sand to cover a dead camel. You won't have to sleep out a storm more than a few days at worst. Remember sandstorms are not blizzards. Your real danger is getting lost by traveling in zero visibility.

Sunglare and dark glasses. The color of the ground varies a great deal in different deserts. In areas where there is light sand as much as 80 percent of the light which falls on it is reflected back. That is getting near the amount of reflection from snow.

"Snow-blindness" (photophthalmia) is due to the reflection of short wave length ultraviolet light. Since there is a little higher percentage of ultraviolet light in equatorial regions, there is probably a damaging concentration of these light rays at eye level from the reflected light in some desert regions.

Solar retinitis produced by the short infrared and visible light rays can also occur in deserts. You won't be bothered by this, however, unless you look at the sun or are scanning the sky in the area immediately adjacent to the sun.

All of which means that sunglasses of some sort are good for you. Even though the glare does not seem painful to you the very high light intensities of the desert will cause a decrease in your night vision.

Regular flying sunglasses in large frames are the easy and satisfactory solution to the problem of sunglare. Lenses should be preferably neutral density lenses of 12-16 percent transmission. They should be large to prevent light from the sides from striking the eye. Such glasses will be some protection against dust, but by no means complete protection.

If you do not have sunglasses, make slit goggles of cloth as described in AFM 64-5. It also helps to shade the eyes with a hat or a turban that has cloth down the sides of your face.

SHELTER

Natural shelter in the Sahara or Gobi is limited to the shade of cliffs or of steep hills. In some desert mountains you can find good cave-like protection under the tumbled blocks of rocks broken from cliff sides. Rarely you may find a twisted, stunted bush or tree to spread your parachute over for shade, but shelter out on the open plains, like food and water, you must carry with you.

A camp in summer desert is cooler on sand than among rocks. Sand loses heat fast. Rocks hold it and can be oven-hot far into the night. During Sahara winter (October to May) the absence of shelter is not serious. Nights are cold, but not much below freezing, while daytime temperatures reach the eighties and low nineties. You will not suffer from exposure if properly dressed.

The summer months bring hot days, and shelter from the midday sun is advisable. Natives on desert journeys carry tents either of skins or of woven wool cloth. They also carry their tent poles and stakes. These tents are about 4 feet high in the center, sloping to about 18 inches above the ground. During the heat of the day this gives good circulation of air and a cool place to rest. When it begins to get too cool in late afternoon or evening, matting is unrolled around the inside edge of the tent to stop the breeze and make the tent warm. Some nomad groups raise and lower the edges of the tent as the temperature rises and falls.

In Sahara oases, dwellings are of adobe, thick-walled, flat-roofed, and often are whitewashed and painted blue around the windows and doors. Blue reduces the glare and seems to keep away some of the flies.

The Gobi Mongols use semipermanent circular dwellings called *yurts*. These are made by lashing a thick sheet of felt around a willow or bamboo frame. The conical roof is also of felt and has an open smoke hole like an American Indian tepee.

Mongol lamaseries are adobe structures built for them by Chinese laborers and decorated with red and gold. Many lamas, however, erect felt yurts in temple courtyards for their sleeping quarters. The felt yurt, like the adobe house, is well insulated against both the summer heat and the winter cold. The latter is a serious hazard in the Gobi, where January and February temperatures are regularly down to 15 or 20 degrees below zero, Fahrenheit.

For light travel, especially in summer, the Mongols use a light cotton cloth tent. This is blue outside and white inside. It is an A-type tent, also sloping to the ground at both front and back. Like the circular yurt, it offers minimum wind resistance. Tent poles and pegs are carried with the cloth, as no supports are available in the desert. During hot middays of July and August the edges of the tent are propped

Mongol women of Chahar, Inner Mongolia. The costumes of these women show considerable Chinese influence; the headdresses, however, are distinctly characteristic of Mongolia. The semipermanent dwellings or yurts of the Mongols are composed of felt layers lashed to portable wood frames. Note that the smoke hole may be covered from different sides in accordance with wind direction. The yurt offers minimum resistance to wind and is well insulated against both desert heat and desert cold.

up to allow free circulation of air. When strong winds blow, extra ropes over ridge pole and sides are staked down to keep the tent from ballooning off across the desert.

DESERT FIRES AND FUEL

Cooking fires are not large in the Sahara, and it is rare, not over a day or two at a time in winter, that a fire is needed to warm the adobe houses of oases. In the houses of wealthy natives, where floors are covered with rugs, fires are built in various types of braziers. In ordinary houses and in caravan and nomad camps, fire is built on the ground.

Stems of palm leaves and similar wood serve as fuel in and near oases. Out on the open desert dry roots or any bit of dead vegetation are carefully hoarded to boil tea or cook a meal. Dried camel dung is the standard fuel where woody fibers are lacking.

In the Gobi, dried heifer dung is the preferred fuel. You will recognize it by the symmetrical shape in contrast to the broad irregular pattern of cow dung. It burns with a hot blue flame in contrast to the smoky yellow flame of cow dung, sheep droppings, etc. Bricks of hand-pressed dung are used to build winter corrals, and as the cold becomes severe the top layers of the corral walls are used as fuel for cooking and for heating the yurts. *Argol* is the Mongol word for all kinds of dung. The natives have large argol baskets and argol forks which are used in collecting animal droppings for winter fuel supply.

DESERT CLOTHING

In summer heat, desert conditions call for head and body covering against direct sunlight and excessive evaporation of sweat. Natives in the Sahara prefer white, either wool or cotton. Even the Tuaregs, who are famous for their blue-black garments and face veils, wear white cotton undergarments all the time and white outer garments on occasion.

Gobi natives wear dark clothing, even in summer, and in winter add sheepskin overcoats. Gobi winters are cold, and bitter winds are common. During that season you will be comfortable if dressed as you would be for a Dakota winter. In spring and fall, the strong wind and dust penetrate ordinary clothing so that a sheepskin-lined garment is comfortable even though the temperature is not much below freezing.

During Sahara winters, natives wrap themselves in woolen burnooses or capes with hoods. Explorers often dress in woolen underwear, wool riding trousers, wool shirts, and sheepskin coats. By 10 o'clock in the morning, the coat is removed; by 1 p.m., the wool shirt is open at the neck and sleeves are rolled up. At 4 p.m. the process is reversed, and before long the wool-lined coat is welcomed again.

Camel riders in the Sahara wear sandals. They protect the feet against stones and the hot desert ground in summer. They are easily removed and hung on camel saddles while the rider's bare feet rest on the camel's neck. Oasis dwellers wear low-cut shoes or slippers easily removed before entering a dwelling, whether it be tent, adobe house, or Mohammedan mosque.

The Gobi Mongols wear high leather boots with curious turned-up toes. They are not designed for walkathon contestants, but then a Mongol won't walk 50 feet if a horse is available, and he sees to it that one is always tied in front of his yurt.

In either desert a good hiking boot which is comfortable and suited to the taste of the wearer is the best footgear for an American who finds himself afoot. Desert surfaces are not often as hard as concrete, although there are many rock plateaus in Sahara and Gobi. A good leather or composition sole will protect your feet from gravel and bunch grass-covered surfaces. Generally, loose trouser legs will be more comfortable than wraps or puttees in summer. That again varies with individuals. Some men

definitely like high leather boots or leather puttees even though they are hot in summer.

Sand dune areas can be crossed barefoot in cool weather but in hot summer weather any desert surface will burn the soles of your feet unless you are a professional fire walker. The average man will sink down in the sand less than an inch when walking across dunes barefooted or with shoes. With broad-soled sandals, a little sand occasionally spills onto the top until you become accustomed to handling them. Sand does slow your speed somewhat, compared to the level plains, but it is not a particular handicap. Neither is it a condition requiring special preparation for keeping sand out of your shoes, as some survival literature would indicate.

DESERT TRAVEL

The great deserts of the Old World have been crossed and recrossed for hundreds and thousands of years. These crossings follow definite routes along marked trails from oasis to wells and wells to water holes or other oases. In the course of centuries some routes have been abandoned when easier routes were discovered. Who dug the wells? Who planned the first crossing? These are questions not often answered, but sometimes there are explanations in historic records or legends.

In some areas governments have provided for keeping wells open or digging new wells, but most desert travelers are public-spirited enough to fix a well that needs repairs. Their generosity doesn't extend to leaving a rope for the next traveler. Unless you are agile enough to go down and up a chimney like Santa Claus, you had better carry a hundred-foot rope in the Sahara. Thirty feet will reach water in most Gobi wells.

Bandits and smugglers, especially in Asia, often search out old abandoned routes and even dig new wells to make difficult trails usable. Changes in governments and political boundaries sometimes produce confiscatory customs stations on desert routes. Then caravans abandon the easy trails in favor of tough-going routes in friendly territory.

Desert trails are visible from the air. They lead to native settlements and wells or water holes, which are located along their route. Note the patch work fields of dry farming on this edge of the Syrian Desert.

Desert trails resemble interlacing cow paths, all leading in the same general direction. Usually these networks of paths are only a few yards wide. In rough terrain there may be two or three paths close together, but in a pasture or region of some vegetation the trail may be half a mile wide. In either case trails are usually as clear and distinct as the cow paths in a farm lane. They can be seen easily from an automobile or from the air.

In Algerian Sahara trail junctions are often marked with wooden signposts giving distances. Automobile routes are frequently well outlined with pebbles, for the trail makers actually swept the surface of the desert to mark the route. Gasoline pumps and rest houses have also been erected all across the Sahara, but they are supplied only when the tourist busses are expected.

Automobile routes in the Sahara do not always follow the camel routes. Frequently the auto trails traverse more barren country where water holes are great distances apart, while camel routes generally strike water every 20 to 40 miles. In the extremely dry Tanezroufts and in Tripoli there are waterless stretches of over 100 miles, but these are rare.

In dune areas wind soon obliterates camel tracks, but the trail can be followed by watching the accumulation of camel droppings in hollows just below the dune crests. On the open plain automobile tracks remain visible for years after a car has passed.

Caravan trails in Mongolia are well marked by piles of stones 6 to 10 feet high placed like lighthouses on prominent buttes and mesa edges. They are called *obos* and serve the double purpose of sign posts to travelers and religious monuments. Some have small openings in the stone structure where once a year the Mongol lamas place food for the spirits who inhabit the area. This is done at the time of

Mongols in characteristic costume. Like other desert dwellers, their bodies are well protected against heat and cold by loosefitting garments. Note the turned-up toes to Mongol boots, footgear not designed for walkathon contests.

An obo is a combination religious monument and lighthouse in the Gobi of Mongolia. Located on a high point it is built of stones and can be seen for considerable distance. Once a year food for the spirits is placed in the little opening among the rocks. Pieces of cloth with sacred significance are draped above the obo to flutter in the wind and carry prayers aloft. As each obo differs from all others in structure passing caravans use them as guideposts in their travels.

a religious feast when the obo is decorated with silk prayer cloths. Desert winds soon whip the silk to shreds, but some bits of cloth will cling to the strings on the monument until the next ceremony and will waft lama prayers aloft to desert gods.

Transportation in both the Gobi and the Sahara has been by camel caravan for centuries. Where distances between wells or watering places are not more than 1 day's march in the Sahara, the horse and little donkey are considered more speedy than the camel. Those animals must be watered twice a day, however, which forces them to give way on long dry marches to the slower, more cantankerous camel, who isn't even inconvenienced by a 2 to 4 days' jaunt between drinks.

Cumbersome two-wheeled ox carts covered with matting to protect the freight from rain and snow lurch over many Gobi trails from June to snowfall (late August or September). Plodding oxen and heavy wheels cut deep into Gobi grasslands when rain soaks the trail. Then the route may be half or three-quarters of a mile wide, and motor cars swing wide from the trail to avoid the ruts.

In both the Sahara and the Gobi, as well as in much of the American desert country, travel by ordinary automobile is practical. Where the route leads down off a mesa or where it crosses a dry wash, it is often wise to follow the "road." Otherwise, one can drive almost anywhere and even chase antelope with a car.

That does not apply to mountainous areas, sand dune regions, or badlands, which exist in parts of all deserts. You may have to detour such places or be very selective of your path, but in general motorcars will take you where you want to go faster than camels or your own two feet.

Desert mountains are common throughout the Arabian Peninsula. Stunted trees and scanty vegetation in the mountains offer more shelter than one finds on the open desert.

Natives of the deserts have little idea of distances. Once in the Sahara an American asked a sheik how far it was to the next oasis.

"Seventy-five kilometers," said the Arab.

"But we have an automobile," said the American, thinking perhaps that the camel route would be too rough and the car would have to detour.

"Oh, with an automobile it is only 25 kilometers," replied the sheik. Time and distance are thoroughly mixed in the native concept. To the sheik kilometers are not a standard of measurable distance. They are just a way of expressing how long it takes to travel from here to there. Don't take a native's statement of distance too seriously, but if he tells you how many days it will take you to walk to the next well, he will state the time with accuracy.

Caravans travel at night in summer if visibility is adequate. They also travel in the early morning or late afternoon. In hot weather they almost never travel after 10 a.m. and before 5 or 6 p.m. There is more daytime travel in winter. Traveling at night, a large caravan may pass close by without your seeing it. If your ears are keen, however, you will hear the creak of boxes on camel saddles or the swish and whispered rustle of rubbing bales and bags.

Walking is not at all difficult in deserts. Caravan men walk as much as they ride and frequently wear only light sandals. Trails avoid the difficult terrain like loose sand or broken rocky areas.

Sand dune pattern in the Western Erg of Algerian Sahara near the oasis of Timmimoun. Prevailing wind direction is from upper right to lower left. Flat basins between the dunes are often suitable for emergency landing. These basins tend to be located in patterns associated with prevailing wind direction. Note the corner of an oasis at right center on a basin edge. Scattered date palm trees are in dune hollows in lower center. Wells are frequently located in the middle of flat basins among the dunes.

If you cannot follow a trail, your best bet is to head for the coast, providing you know where it is and the distance is within range of your strength and water supply. Once you reach the coast you can conserve your sweat by soaking your clothes in the sea.

Valleys, ancient stream beds or dry water courses lead to inland basins in desert areas. In Libyan Sahara such valleys start within a few hundred yards of the sea and run inland. Great, through-going rivers like the Nile, Tigris and Euphrates, the Rio Grande and Colorado which carry water all year do reach the sea of course. Even some short valleys join the ocean, but you better have a map to guide you in any generalization about following stream beds or valleys in the desert.

Maps of desert regions are notoriously bad. They serve to give you a general idea of terrain features but often specific landmarks are located 50 miles in error. Try to get an estimated accuracy from a reliable source for any map you carry, check that accuracy *before* you have to use the map.

Orientation. In the air or on the ground it is not easy to orient yourself in the desert. There are few check points. Distances are deceiving. The landscape is monotonous, and the features of one area often resemble those of a distant region. The sun is not much help in a duststorm or a coastal desert fog. Mirages distort even middle distance landmarks and sometimes cause you to lose sight of others.

You can improve your ability to orient yourself by consciously identifying those features of the landscape your eyes encounter. Practice looking at known objects distorted by mirages.

One or two attempts to look carefully at familiar objects in a duststorm or a whiteout will convince you of the need for training yourself in desert observation and of the importance of "waiting for the sunshine" in an emergency.

Signaling. The Siamese twins of desert survival are water and signaling. Their importance was emphasized in 1955 by widely publicized desert emergencies in southwest United States. In each case proper signaling equipment or a little more water would have averted tragedy. (Water is discussed in the next chapter.)

The Air Force provides emergency radio equipment. Learn to use it properly. Learn its capabilities before you need it. Then check before you take off to be sure the battery is not dead. A dead radio in a desert emergency can mean a dead pilot.

If you have no radio, you can indicate your position in the desert to search planes by visual signals. A pillar of smoke by day, a column of fire by night are excellent, but a mirror's blinding flash by day and a battery flashlight at night will do the job. You may have to provide your own flashlight, but the Air Force survival equipment includes an excellent signal mirror. Learn to use it so the pilot will not confuse your signal with a gun flash—hold it on him until he turns toward you. Don't blind him when he is trying to help you. Pilots say the mirror's light can "knock you out of the cockpit," so after you are sure you have been seen, don't overdo it.

DAYS of EXPECTED SURVIVAL in the DESERT

Under Two Conditions

No Walking at all.

Max. Daily Shade Temp° F.	Available Water per Man, U.S. Quarts					
	0	1	2	4	10	20
	Days of Expected Survival					
120°	2	2	2	2.5	3	4.5
110°	3	3	3.5	4	5	7
100°	5	5.5	6	7	9.5	13.5
90°	7	8	9	10.5	15	23
80°	9	10	11	13	19	29
70°	10	11	12	14	20.5	32
60°	10	11	12	14	21	32
50°	10	11	12	14.5	21	32

Walking at night until exhausted and resting thereafter.

Max. Daily Shade Temp° F.	Available Water per Man, U.S. Quarts					
	0	1	2	4	10	20
	Days of Expected Survival					
120°	1	2	2	2.5	3	
110°	2	2	2.5	3	3.5	
100°	3	3.5	3.5	4.5	5.5	
90°	5	5.5	5.5	6.5	8	
80°	7	7.5	8	9.5	11.5	
70°	7.5	8	9	10.5	13.5	
60°	8	8.5	9	11	14	
50°	8	8.5	9	11	14	

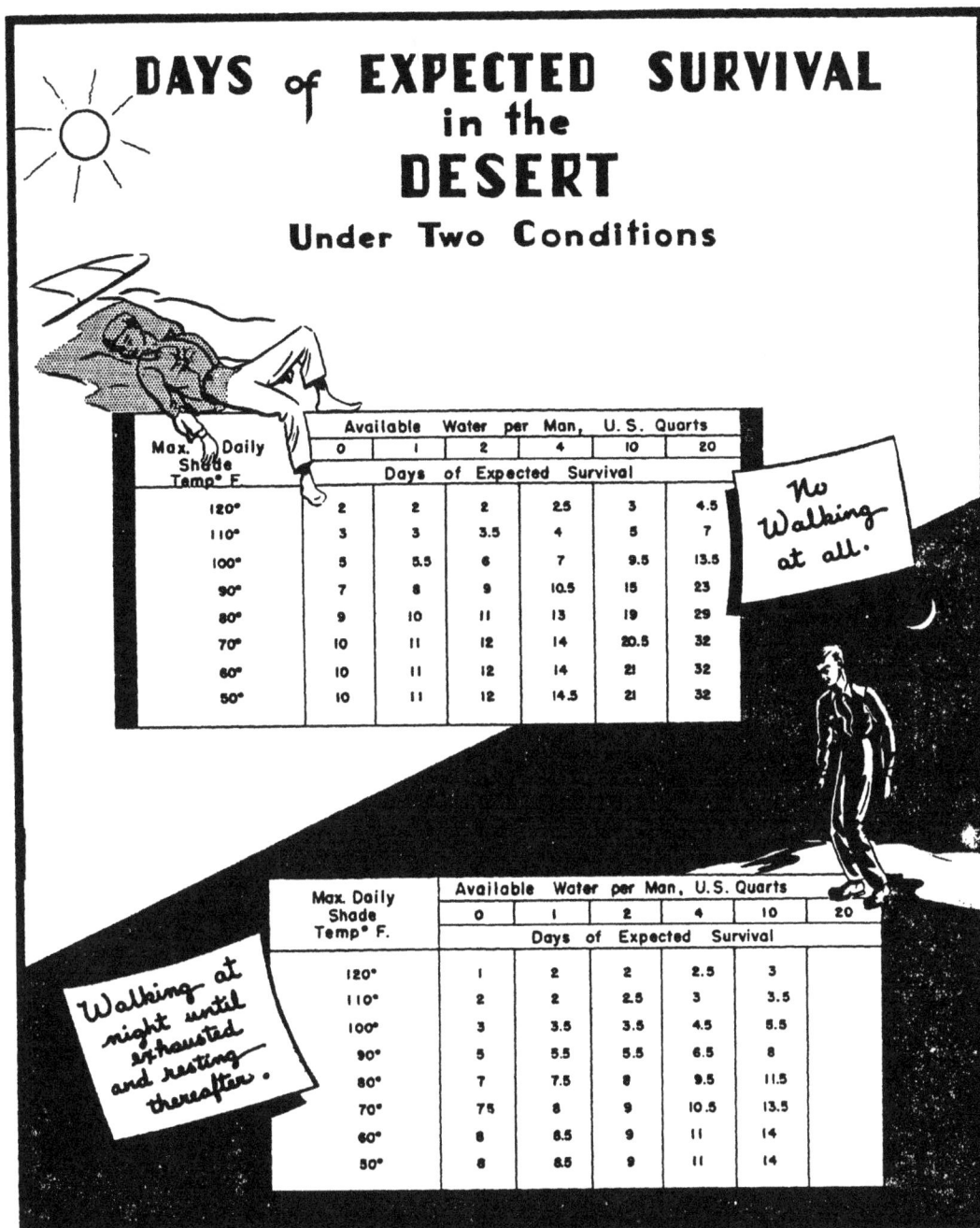

This is Table 17B, p. 279, in **Physiology of Man in the Desert,** by E. F. Adolph and Associates, New York: Interscience Publishers, 1947. Note that survival time is not appreciably increased until available water is about 4 quarts, the amount necessary to maintain water balance for 1 day at high temperatures. Utilization of shade or saving a few degrees of temperature is as effective and as important in increasing survival time as water.

Water needs in the jungle are much less than in the desert. At equal temperatures the body requires two to three times as much water to maintain water balance in deserts as it does in jungles.

PART IV

WATER: THE SECRET OF STRENGTH AND EFFICIENCY
—HOW TO USE IT IN HOT DESERTS

THE NORMAL body temperature for man is 98.6°. Any variation, even as little as one or two degrees from that normal temperature, reduces your efficiency.

Patients have survived after a few minutes of body temperature as low as 20 degrees below normal (78.8° and 75.2°).[12] However, their consciousness became clouded at half that drop in temperature.

In contrast, an increase in body temperature of six to eight degrees above normal for any extended period causes death. This fact is familiar to everyone. When sickness or disease causes the body temperature to go above the normal 98.6, we call it fever. High fever can burn up the patient so that in the case of sickness, efforts are directed to keeping the body temperature within bounds.

Body temperature in a healthy person also can be raised to the danger point either by absorbing heat or by generating heat too fast. The body absorbs heat from the air if the air is above 92°F. It can get it from direct sunlight striking the body, radiant heat, even if the air is relatively cool. It can absorb heat reflected from the ground or it can absorb it direct from the ground by contact, as when you are lying down. Any kind of work or exercise, of course, produces body heat.

Regardless of where the heat comes from, the body must get rid of the excess and keep body temperature at the normal 98.6°. This is done by evaporating sweat on the skin surface. It is a very effective and efficient process.

You can see how effective evaporation is in cooling if you fill a desert water bag and a canteen with water and hang them both in the sun. When the water in the canteen is 110°F, the water in the sweating desert bag will be only 70°F. Evapora-

tion of sweat on the desert bag keeps it 40° cooler. Evaporation of sweat on your skin keeps your body temperature normal.

When you sweat, however, your body loses water. That is called dehydration. It is true that two-thirds of the human body is water, but every bit of body water is needed for circulation! Therefore when you lose body water by sweating, when you dehydrate, that loss must be replaced by drinking water. Otherwise the body pays for the loss in reduced efficiency. Actual, scientifically controlled experiments on men working in hot deserts have given us some figures on loss of efficiency compared to the percent of dehydration or loss of body water.

For instance, a man who has lost 2½ percent of his body weight by sweating (about 2 quarts of water) loses 25 percent of his efficiency. Also it has been found that working in air temperatures of 110° cuts down a man's normal ability about 25 percent. That means that if your body is short 1½ quarts of water and the air around you is 110°F, you are only half a man. You can do only about half as much work as you normally do. You can walk only half as far as you could with plenty of water in normal temperatures.

Most people can get accustomed to working in high temperatures, whether in the stokehold of a ship or in a harvest field on the Kansas prairie. It may take a good man from 2 days to a week before his circulation, his breathing, his heart action, and his sweat glands all get tuned to hot climate work. Some people never do adjust to hot weather; others adjust quickly. Some people even have more sweat glands per square inch of skin surface than others. Extra glands help them acclimatize more quickly. It has been found that those brought up from infancy in hot climates really do have more sweat glands than people raised in temperate climates.

[12]Dorothy Mae (Johny) Stevens, 23-year-old Chicago Negro girl survived a body temperature of 64.4° in 1951, but eventually lost both legs.

Although your body may acclimatize to hot weather, it must have water to form sweat and supply liquid for circulation. When the body dehydrates, the blood loses more than its share of water. Blood becomes thicker and less in volume. The result is more work for the heart and less efficiency in circulation.

Most people drink the liquid they need at meal times. In hot climates they tend to dehydrate between meals and are restored to normal when they eat and drink. Such people often claim that they are tired when in reality their loss of energy is due to dehydration.

Efficiency loss by dehydration is quickly restored by drinking water. Replacing water lost by sweating will in a few minutes restore a man who has collapsed from dehydration. That means you can keep your efficiency in summer desert weather by drinking plenty of water. Without water in hot deserts you will not travel far. The product of your labor will be small.

It is important to remember that there is no permanent harm done to a man who dehydrates even up to 10 percent of his weight. If you weigh 150 pounds, you can sweat off 15 pounds *if* you drink enough water to gain it back later.[13] You probably would not be able to walk to the drinking fountain if you dehydrated that much. If you could stagger over there and drink a quart or two of cool water, you would be back on your feet in a few minutes; ready to battle the champion, as soon as you had replaced all the lost water. Ice cold water, however, may cause stomach distress if drunk too rapidly, but warm or cool water may be swallowed as fast as you like.

There is no evidence that anyone can acclimatize to dehydration.[14] Some men have been dehydrated 15 or 20 times under experimental conditions. *It took just as much water to bring them back to normal effi-*

ciency after the last dehydration as it did after the first. During their dehydration the same symptoms, the same loss of efficiency always occurred at the same stages or percentage of water loss.

Here's how you feel when you dehydrate. First you are thirsty and uncomfortable. Then you start taking it easy, sort of slow motion, and have no appetite. As you lose more water, you get sleepy, your temperature goes up, and by the time you are dehydrated to 5 percent of your body weight, you get sick at your stomach.

From 6 percent to 10 percent dehydration, the symptoms follow in this order:

You experience dizziness, headache, difficulty in breathing, tingling in arms and legs, and a dry mouth; your body gets bluish, your speech is indistinct, and finally you can't walk. From there on you need help, but if you are watching some other fellow with less water than you have, you'll find his symptoms in the tables at the end of this paper.[15] They range from his being off his nut to a numb skin. In any case, get water into him—but quick.

It is probable that man can survive 25 percent dehydration in air temperature of 85°F or cooler. At temperatures up in the nineties and higher, 15 percent dehydration is probably fatal.

The story of Pablo Valencia is a glorious exception.[16] In 1905 Pablo was in the desert of southwestern Arizona for 8 days and nights with 1 day's water. He rode in the saddle for 35 miles and walked or crawled between 100 and 150 miles. For 160 hours he was without water. His arms and legs were cut by thorns and rocks, but his blood was so thick the wounds did not bleed until he was rescued by Dr. McGee and water was gotten into his belly. He lost 25 percent of his weight. During the incident the lowest temperature was 81°F, the maximum

[13]Sven Hedin, the Swedish explorer, once ran out of water. Two of his men died. On reaching water, Hedin drank 6 pints of water at once and was revived without ill effects. His companion who survived drank "two high boots full." Hedin, Sven, *Through Asia*, Harper, 1898, Vols I and II.
Two U.S. aviators who were made prisoners in Italy by the Germans in World War II escaped into an attic and survived 6 days on 1 pint of water. They lay almost inert for fear of recapture and finally fell out of their hiding place. It was several minutes before they could stagger over to water, where they drank 3 pints right away and were able to walk—"Could actually feel energy returning." Personal conversation with survivor at SAC.

[14]Some writers claim that Arabs have acclimatized to dehydration. We find no evidence to support this claim. We do find that desert natives conserve body water by following the rules later stated in this paper; but for equal work in equal temperatures they require as much water as other people. There is a record of two Arab soldiers in the Sahara who were proud of their desert ability and who believed the legend of the desert robber who could go 2 or 3 days without water, just like his camel. These soldiers tried to imitate the legendary hero but collapsed after 36 hours without water. They were revived by drinking water. Gautier, E. F., *Sahara the Great Desert*, New York: Columbia University Press, 1935, tr by D. F. Mayhew.
[15]See Appendix 1.
[16]McGee, Dr. W. J., *Desert Thirst as Disease*. Interstate Medical Journal Vol. XIII No. 3, March, 1906.

103.2 F. Pablo Valencia, however, was out in the open not in the protected shelter of the official thermometer. He was, of course, familiar with the desert trails and dragged himself back to water and help. You can equal Pablo's will to survive. You should outdo him in common sense about water and desert travel.

In summer desert heat, thirst is not a strong enough sensation to indicate the amount of water you need. If you drink only enough to satisfy your thirst, it will still be possible to dehydrate slowly. The best plan is to drink plenty of water any time it is available and particularly at meal times.

There is no substitute for water to prevent dehydration and keep the body at normal efficiency. Alcohol, salt water, gasoline, blood, or urine—any of those liquids which desert and sea castaway romances say men have tried as substitutes for water—*only increase dehydration*. That is because all contain waste products which the body must get rid of through the kidneys. More water is required to carry off the waste through the body than is contained in the liquids mentioned. For example, sea water is more salty than urine; therefore, when sea water is drunk, the body must add more water to carry away the extra salt.

You can drink brackish water—that is water with half as much salt as sea water—and get a net gain of moisture for the body. Any liquid containing a higher percentage of waste than urine can do only harm to your cooling system.

Do not adulterate fresh water! If your fresh water accidently gets mixed with salt, don't waste it. Drink it and get all the possible good from it.

Chewing gum or pebbles in the mouth may be a pleasant form of kidding yourself that you are not thirsty. They do *no harm* but they are not a substitute for water and will not aid in keeping your body temperature normal. Only water, sweated out and evaporated on your skin surface, can do that job. You may smoke, too, if you like. It will not change your need for water.

SALT IN HOT WEATHER

Recent studies on salt needs of the body

indicate that a little extra salt on your food at mealtimes may be necessary for the first few days you are living in hot climates. When you have adjusted to living in the heat, food salted to your taste will supply all your body needs. Unless plenty of water is available, salt will do you definite harm.

Sweat does contain salt, but the body is able to regulate the amount of salt in sweat and so conserve what is needed. In other words, don't worry about your salt but do keep up your water supply.

RATION YOUR SWEAT, NOT YOUR WATER

Your body produces so much heat every hour while at rest that unless that heat is lost, you will have 2 degrees of fever in 1 hour. Evaporating sweat takes care of that heat just as fast as it is formed. In order to keep your body temperature normal, every hundred calories of heat generated by your body and absorbed from air, sun, or ground, must be balanced by the evaporation of 173 grams of sweat.

In hot deserts you need about a gallon of water per day. If you follow the rules and walk in the "cool" desert night, you can get about 20 miles for that daily gallon. If you do your walking in daytime heat, you'll be lucky to get 10 miles to the gallon. Whether you sit out your desert survival or walk home to mother, you'll need water, at least 3 to 4 quarts a day.

The only way to conserve your water is to ration your sweat. Drink your water as you need it, but keep heat out of your body. That can be done if you keep your shirt on. It had better be a white or light-colored shirt. Of course we mean pants, hat, and shoes as well as shirt. Clothing helps ration your sweat by not letting it evaporate so fast that you get only part of its cooling effect. Light clothing also reflects or turns away the heat of the sun and keeps out the hot desert air. Keep in the shade as much as possible during the day. Desert natives have tents open on all sides to allow free circulation of air during the daytime. Sit up a few inches off the ground, if possible; do not lie on the ground. It is 30 to 45 de-

A mirage in the desert resembles this apparent lake on the landing field. The variation in density of air masses causes distortion of light rays so that the image of the sky appears on the ground as a lake. Other distortions cause distant objects like mountains to appear much closer than they really are. Still other conditions produce upside-down images above the horizon. All such distortions are mirages but the apparent-lake type shown above is commonly recognized in deserts.

grees cooler a foot above the ground than it is right on the ground. That difference can save you a lot of sweat.

Slow motion is better than speed in hot deserts. Slow and steady, slow and easy does it. If you must move about in the heat, you'll last longer on less water if you take it easy. Remember the Arab. He is not surviving in the desert; he just lives there—and he likes it. He isn't lazy, he's just living in slow motion, the way the desert makes him live.

If you have plenty of water—2 or 3 gallons per day—go ahead and work your head off if you want to, and drink as often as you like. In fact you had better drink more and oftener than you think your thirst requires, if you want to stay healthy and keep efficient.

You may *feel* more comfortable in the desert without a shirt or pants. That is because your sweat evaporates so fast. But it takes more sweat, and sunburn is a painful trouble. Desert sun will burn even if you have a good coat of tan, so use your head, maintain your efficiency, and keep your clothes on.

DESERTS ARE ALSO COLD

Most people think of deserts as hot, dry, barren wastes where it is a long way between drinks. We have been talking of that type of desert. Heat is a desert characteristic in summer daytime. That is from May to October in the Sahara; during July and August in the Gobi. During the rest of the year you'll need winter clothing in the Sahara and arctic winter clothing in the Gobi.

The distance between wells does not change from summer to winter even if the thermometer does hover in a lower register. You can dehydrate when the temperature is 65° in the shade, but it will take days instead of hours. You need water wherever you are. In desert country you'll find water along trails, so, winter or summer, afoot, on horseback, in a jeep, or aloft in a four-engined aircraft, travel in sight of the trails if not actually on the caravan paths.

JOURNEY OF 1,000 MILES

The Chinese have a saying that a journey of 1,000 miles begins with one step. If you find yourself afoot in the desert, just remember that Chinese have been walking across the deserts of Asia for 2 thousand years. The Arabs have been walking across the Sahara and the Arabian deserts for many centuries. They do it by taking and thinking about just one step at a time. And they follow century-old trails.

All deserts have trails. They are visible from the air. Keep them in sight when you fly the deserts; keep them in mind when you see them on your maps. Land on them if you have any control of your landing.

Trails lead to water. In all deserts, wells, water holes, and oases are reached by trails. In the Gobi wells are often 8, 10, or 15 miles apart. In the Sahara they may be 15 to 40 miles apart. In some sections of both deserts there are longer stretches between wells, but God help you if you come down in regions where there are no trails. Here's hoping you send out a radio fix in any event, but if you are down on a trail you can probably hitchhike to water with a passing caravan. Remember they travel at night in summer heat.

Deserts are big open spaces and a map, even a poor one, will help you locate trails or find water. Don't be without a map and a compass unless you have an Arab's memory for landmarks.

Natives and people who walk the desert trails are friendly people. They know the hardships of the desert, and, like people living close to nature anywhere in the world, their natural sense of hospitality is to help a fellow traveler. That holds particularly true if the stranger appears friendly and is not armed or threatening in his manner.

There are bandits and smugglers in some deserts. The former are usually not far from large centers of population where trails begin to converge. Such groups do not welcome threats or too many questions about their business, but a friendly approach will get you help in the right direction. Of course if you look like a bandit or throw your weight around in the presence of desert travelers, their reaction may be one of self-protection instead of hospitality. A friendly guy afoot in the desert, however, should meet up with friends on the trail.

SUMMARY

Evidence left by those who died of dehydration shows that in temperatures above 100°F you may live a couple of days without water. If you save your energy and keep in the shade, every gallon of water you have means another day of life. Less than 3 quarts of water will not increase your survival time. Rationing yourself to 1 or 2 quarts of water per day at high temperatures is inviting disaster. Such small amounts will not prevent your dehydrating. Loss of efficiency and eventual collapse follow dehydration as surely as night follows day. Ration your sweat, not your water.

There are no substitutes for water, but remember that tea, coffee, milk, fruit juices, and soft drinks are basically water. Pebbles in the mouth, chewing gum, or smoking may make you *feel* better, but they will neither decrease nor increase your need for water. Alcohol, salt water, urine, or any liquid containing quantities of waste material which must be eliminated from the body through the kidneys will increase dehydration. Water in your belly will keep you on your feet in hot summer deserts.

Arabs and Berbers, Mongols and American Indians live and travel in deserts. There are many plants and animals which survive under desert conditions. If you profit by the lessons these desert dwellers have given—if you understand the limitations under which you must walk or wait in the desert—if you practice what we've been preaching, you'll live to know the value of these desert lessons.

The walking is good in deserts. Distances are great, but the obstacles to a man on foot are few. Water is necessary to maintain normal body temperature, and normal temperature is necessary to keep up your efficiency.

In summer desert temperatures you can conserve body water by keeping fully clothed and sitting in the shade during the day. Necessary work or walking should be done at night. Under such conditions in summer a man should be able to travel about 20 miles on a gallon of water. If you work or travel in the heat of daytime deserts, twice or three times as much water is essential to your body.

If you are flying in desert areas, plan to study your maps. Keep in mind the general locations and directions of the trails. Plan now to learn about deserts and desert people. They are interesting. Plan for your water supply if you are in desert areas. Your water needs are great even if you are riding across the desert in a jeep.

It is recorded that one tough general thought troops on desert maneuvers could be toughened to lack of water. A colonel knew better and took the general for a jeep ride with only 2 quarts of water per man. Of course the water lasted the general less than 3 hours. Long before the desert ride was finished, the general was mentally prepared to issue plenty of water to troops on maneuvers. Under hard working conditions in summer daytime desert heat, those troops often used 3 gallons of drinking water per man per day.

The water you drink when exposed to desert heat is not wasted. Carry your water in your belly—drink as you feel thirsty and keep your efficiency. Men have dehydrated with water still in their canteens—and wondered why they couldn't walk or work! It is the water in your body that saves your life, not the water in your canteen.

Start planning your desert walk now. Plan before every take-off for desert flight. Plan on landing and before you start walking. Include water, trails, and friendly natives in all those plans and you can find the desert a fascinating place.

PART V

Oasis and village in the mountains of Morocco. Walled courtyards and flat roofed houses are built of sun-dried brick or adobe. Note the sharp line where the desert meets the irrigated cultivation. The river, almost dry in June, carries considerable water in the winter months.

DESERT PEOPLE AND YOU[17]

PEOPLE who inhabit the great deserts are conservative and pretty well adjusted. In general they have come to terms with nature's elements. They have learned to endure extreme heat in summer and cold in winter. They expect long periods of dryness, and know how to conserve water. They get along with little food, but know how to enjoy a banquet on occasions. They know the limits of the land which can be grazed or used by their family and their tribe. They know who are their friends and who are their enemies. They understand what to expect from both and how to act toward each of them. They know the rules. They believe in those rules and they act in accordance with that belief. Established SOP prevails for most situations.

When an American like you steps into the land of desert people that adjustment is

[17]The Ethnic Card Series being published by ADTIC will give specific details of individual tribes which are beyond the scope of **Afoot in the Desert.** This is ADTIC Publication, G-101.

thrown off balance. The picture is out of focus. The desert native does not know where you fit into his scheme of things. You make confusion in his world. He or she has no idea what to do about you.

What he or she does will depend on several things, but above all else it will probably depend on YOU. If his group has any contact with white-skinned, hat-wearing, trouser-legged individuals like you, he'll treat you according to the pattern his people have decided upon.

If the last shoe-wearing blond he met or has heard about was a natural SOB, the desert man will be expecting trouble. Don't give it to him. If the last friend of democracy the desert people knew was honest, friendly, courteous, a really swell fellow, then your troubles are at a minimum providing you can be as decent.

You can find published books and magazine articles written by desert travelers which call the natives treacherous, vicious, sly, hostile, and dangerous. Most of those authors had already formed their opinion before they reached the desert. Some of them wanted to prove how brave they were in going into "a land of terror." Some newcomers got into trouble and never knew why. Often it was because they had violated some simple customs like putting out the wrong hand. Others boast of how they gyped the natives. Many went looking for trouble "with a gun on each hip and chip on each shoulder." Naturally the desert people were on guard against such unfriendly or arrogant intruders.

Arabs are exchangers of gifts. Gifts represent friendship. If you learn what simple presents you can give in your particular section of Sahara or Arabia you can get more cooperation than money can buy.

The author once gave a Swiss jackknife to a Tuareg noble in the Sahara. It cost 50 cents in the States. Later he received courtesies out of all proportion to the demands of hospitality. Finally the noble explained. "When you first came here you gave me a knife that closes. All my life I have wanted a knife that closes. You are my friend. Anything I have is yours."

The Bedouin you are likely to meet on the Sahara and Arabian deserts have a really hard life. They have little food and few clothes in a rugged climate. Cash money is hard to come by, and it is usable in many ways.

He will do a great many things for money, but money will not tempt him to sacrifice his honor. He sticks rigidly to his code.

A man's first duty is towards God.

Second: the protection of his tent neighbor.

Third: attention to the laws of hospitality.

Fourth: duty to a traveler under his "safe conduct."

Fifth: attention to the laws of personal protection and sanctuary.

Sixth: is duty to himself; to raid when he can and to keep what he has captured.

Raiding is no sin but a virtue. Payment, you might say, for the five good deeds above. To kill your enemy is a greater virtue. To steal your enemy's cattle isn't robbery; it is something to be proud of. Your enemy will do the same to you if you give him a chance.

Some Americans and other non-natives have gone among the desert people as friends. They have lived among them as equals. Those who have treated the desert people as decently and honestly as they would treat their friends at home all agree that desert people are hospitable, dignified and friendly.

This author once went down into the Hoggar Mountains of the Algerian Sahara on a civilian expedition. Expedition members heard so many tales of treachery and ambush by the Tuaregs that a machine gun was carried on one of the cars in addition to side arms and rifles. On the northern edge of the desert we stopped at a French military post. Among other questions, we asked about our machine gun.

"It is excellent for shooting Gazelles," said the Commandant, "but if you want to shoot Tuaregs, extra film for your camera will be more practical."

We left the machine gun with the Commandant and found the Tuaregs so friendly that they enjoyed our singing "Old MacDonald Had a Farm." They joined us in wrestling matches and even invited us to an Ahal. That is not a subject for publication.

Experienced desert travelers have found that an honest effort to understand the desert people pays off. A sincere respect for their customs, no matter how different from yours they may be, will result in satisfactory relationships all around. That applies even in the exceptional regions where groups or individuals may be hostile or trigger happy.

Remember when you enter the land of desert people, you are the foreigner in another's home town. It is up to you to act in accordance with their customs. When you are the foreigner, act with the decency you'd expect of a foreigner in your home. Act like an undesirable, and your sweetheart may be looking for another boy friend.

Photo by Carleton S. Coon.

A Ga' inat village of Khunik Pai Godar in the Khorasan desert region of Iran. Dome-roofed buildings and irrigated terraces are characteristic of this arid part of the Near East.

Among desert people if you give your word you must keep it. In Saudi Arabia the courts will see that you do keep your verbal agreements. For example, if you say you will pay a certain price for a rug and later see another which you like better you can't back out of your first verbal deal even though you have not paid anything down nor taken delivery.

The people of Saudi Arabia can't understand our custom of signing a written agreement and having witnesses sign. They give their word and keep their verbal promises.

Desert people are not fist fighters. They don't lay violent hands on each other in anger or in horseplay, as youthful Americans sometimes do. To inflict physical injury on an Arab, for example, is a very serious offence. You may find yourself legally obliged to support the injured and his family.

Article 39 of the Saudi Arabian laws prohibits you from striking a person by hand or by tongue or from treating him with scorn or contempt.

There are many very interesting angles to the customs of desert people, and in well organized Saudi Arabia many of those old customs are written into law.

Here are a few of the most important don'ts. In general they apply to the deserts everywhere.

- Don't bawl out an offender in front of other people.
- Don't draw sand pictures or maps with your foot. Stoop down and draw with right hand.
- Don't swear at a native.
- Don't expose the soles of your feet to others. Sit tailor fashion or on your heels.
- Don't ask about a man's wife.
- Don't throw a coin at a man's feet, that is insulting.
- Gambling is forbidden.
- DO HAVE PATIENCE when dealing with desert people.
- DO ACT FRIENDLY.

Customs differ in different desert regions They differ sometimes between tribes of the same region. For instance, some natives we have met in the Gobi stuck out their tongue as a "hello" type of greeting. Later we learned it was more characteristic of Tibet than Mongolia. Others in Mongolia extended the right hand as a fist but with the thumb up. The same sign was used to ask the expedition physician if the patient would get well. In the Algerian Sahara a lone traveler often advanced to meet us with his right hand raised like the traditional American Indian pose when saying "How." Others extended the right hand to touch ours almost like a simple handshake. There was no firm grip and shake but just a touch of the right palms. Then each man put the back of his hand to his lips.

These are just a few of the greeting customs of desert people. *Afoot in the Desert* is not large enough to give the customs of all groups. Its purpose is to give you general ideas of what customs to look for. With this background you should catch on quickly to the local Emily Post recommendations in any desert. Learn the customs for your region. When a man shakes his fist at you, he may be saying, "Hello Friend."

In some parts of the Gobi you should only approach a yurt or a tent from the east. That will be the front where the only door is located. If you happen to come from some other direction, you should circle the yurt at a reasonable distance. Give the Mongols a chance to see you before you get close to their dwelling.

In Mongolia dogs will probably warn of your approach. Then you'll need a club or some stones to keep them at bay while you shout to the inhabitants, "Call off the dogs." Learn the proper words in the native language of the desert you are traveling. Women, girls or anyone else around will come out and quiet the animals.

You enter the yurt through the left side of the door. You leave your whip or club outside above the door. There are rules regarding what part of the yurt is reserved for each member of the family and for guests. Your good nature and friendliness, however, will get you by until you know the rules.

Some Mongols are extremely informal and enter without knocking. The author remembers one time when a Mongol woman walked into his tent without knocking or calling. She sat on the ground for 10 minutes in front of him while he proceeded with his allover sponge bath. She had passed the prime of her youth and beauty, and she needed a bath worse than the author, so the experience didn't raise his blood pressure.

In Arabia the guest must also approach the tent from the front. Front will be in the lee of the wind. If the wind changes, the back will be raised and become the front. Stop some distance away to give the gals time to get their veils in place. During summer heat all sides of the tent will be raised so you better observe the people from a distance to be sure which is front.

On the edge of the Sahara in Algeria it is customary to call out on approaching a tent. This is particularly true if there are no men around. In that region the author did not enter the tent unless invited. Curiously Americans were welcomed, and they were allowed to photograph the Berber nomad women. A cousin of the family who acted as interpreter could not come near the tent. Necessary interpreting was conducted by shouting back and forth.

Don't surprise people in the desert if you expect their help or hospitality. Their reaction to surprise may be a disappearing act. It may also be a hostile reception especially if you are in bandit country.

In some sections of the Arabian Desert and in some parts of the Sahara a guest will be welcomed with a bowl of milk. In Arabia (Dickson says) "it will be buttermilk." In the Algerian Sahara the writer has always been offered sheep or goats milk and a tray of dates. In the Gobi it was a piece of stone-hard cheese. In parts of the Arabian Desert, when the man of the tent is away, his wife will welcome a passing group. If she has reason to believe that the approaching group is led by the Sheik or other important personage, she hangs out her best dress as a banner on a pole by the tent.

Set phrases of welcome and greeting are repeated and answered in all regions. Learn those used in your region. Even if you pronounce the phrases badly your effort will be appreciated. It may even cause some merriment among your hosts and that always increases friendliness.

The believers of Islam in North Africa, Arabia, and the deserts of Central Asia consider hospitality an important duty. The traveler in those regions accepts that hospitality naturally. However, gentlemanly instincts are highly developed even among the poorer desert men. They approach a tent "modestly and with becoming diffidence" and call out a friendly greeting like "salam alaikum" (peace be upon you). A guest would never dream of offering payment for his accommodations and such an offer would not be accepted. Neither would the guest think of imposing on the hospitality of a neighbor if he could make it to his own tent.

Photo by Dr. Wm. M. Shanklin.

Camp of Emir Fawaz Shalan in the Syrian Desert near Palmyra. The Emir is head of the Rwala Tribe. Camps are never as large as this in the Sahara.

Three days is the limit one should stay in a host's tent. A longer stay is not only bad manners, but it permits the host to urge you to continue on your journey.

The rule of hospitality is so rigid that it could easily cause the ruin of a poor man if his tent was located on a main trail. Those who are poor accordingly often hide their camp in a hollow or behind a hill away from traveled routes. They dare not refuse hospitality even to a stranger although feeding him may force them to go without. Their best bet is to keep their camp hard to find. Your best bet is to look for a side trail leading off behind a hill. It may lead to hospitality.

Religion among desert people ranges from fanatical adherence to rigid forms through dignified sincerity to the most casual lip service.

Among Gobi Mongols two-thirds of the male population were lamas or priests of Lamaism. Most westerners consider Lamaism a decadent form of Buddhism. Certainly it has absorbed a great many local spirits, and the common people were imposed upon by the lamas through serious superstitions which they kept alive. The largest collections of permanent buildings in Mongolia were the lamasaries. Since the region has been controlled by the soviets the number of lamas has been greatly reduced. It is thought that they now include only 3 percent of the male population instead of the former 60 percent. Probably the average Mongol should be considered more superstitious than religious. The soviets have reduced the power of the lamas, but it is doubtful if they have eliminated superstition.

Among the Arabs of Arabia and the Sahara many of the tribes are really sincere. They truly believe in one God. They do not need anyone to intercede for them but each man prays direct to God. This he does with dignity, secure in the knowledge that before God he stands on an equal footing with every other man.

The true believer in the Moslem religion knows that there is no God but God and Mohammed was his Prophet.

He says his prayers five times each day. He gives alms to the poor and needy. During the month of Ramadhan he does not eat, drink nor have sexual intercourse between sunrise and sunset, but he can and does indulge during the night. If his means permit, he will make the journey to Mecca at least once in his lifetime. This is becoming easier to do now that airlines in the Near East can fly the pilgrims to Jidda.

The believer in Islam prefers to be called a Moslem. Remember that while he knows that Mohammed was the Prophet of God, the Moslem does not worship Mohammed. It is, therefore, not correct to call him a Mohammedan.

A Moslem can and does worship wherever he is. When prayer time comes, he will stop whatever he is doing, face Mecca and go through the seven positions of prayer while he repeats set phrases and suras from the Koran. That applies out in the desert or in the lobby of an office building in the city.

In cities and in oases there are mosques where Moslems go to pray and to meditate. In the courtyard or somewhere near the entrance will be a place for the believer to wash his hands and feet before entering the religious sanctuary. He always removes his shoes or sandals before entering the mosque. You will show the same courtesy and remove your shoes. In tourist cities extra sandals are sometimes provided for non-Moslems who are visiting the holy places. Put these on over your shoes. In the desert you may not be allowed inside the mosque at all but don't defile the holy place with your shoes if you are allowed to enter. The offense is serious in some places, and may start a riot against you.

Many desert people are superstitious about photographs. They rationalize their fear by saying that the Koran forbids pictures. There is no such ban on pictures in the Moslem religious book, but it will do you no good to try to argue the matter. In Damascus the author has been urged by his guide in a mosque "to take all the pictures you want." In the same city, however, individuals objected violently to any photographs even out on the street.

Photo by Standard Oil Co. (N. J.)

A Bedouin in prayer position before his tent in Nedj, Saudi Arabia.

You will have to learn the "temper" of the desert people you encounter and follow their taboos. Respect their prejudices. Don't ridicule or make fun of desert people. All of them are proud people. They are following customs that have proved satisfactory to them for more centuries than your ways have years.

Women among desert people have varied positions. Except among the very wealthy families, all desert women do their share of work about the camp. In Mongolia there is no double standard of morals. Among the Arabs most tribes do not allow their women to show their faces to any men except the closest members of the family. In contrast to this strict seclusion the women of tribes just north of Yemen on the Arabian Peninsula "expose more of their bodies than would be tolerated in other parts of Arabia." They have greater freedom and freer intercourse with men than in the more puritani-

cal districts of Arabia proper. Philby[18] also relates that he saw young, well-formed women bathing in a stream. Each showed neither shame nor embarrassment. Others exposed their "well-formed breasts," and one took off her shawl, which was her only garment, in order to rearrange it.

Most Arabs and Berber peoples of Arabia or the Great Sahara tolerate no nonsense between their women and men to whom they are not married. Violations of the code brings swift, sure punishment, sometimes including the death of the woman.

In contrast the Tuaregs of Sahara pride themselves on the complete absence of jealousy. The women go unveiled before all men while the men never show their faces even in all male gatherings. Their Ahal gatherings include young married and unmarried men and women. They play the

[18]Philby, H. St. J. B., Arabian Highlands. The Middle East Institute, Washington, D. C., 1952, Pages 275, 447, 451, 456, and others.

Photo by Standard Oil Co. (N. J.)

A Bedouin with his wives and children in front of his tent at Abqaiq, Al Hasa, Saudi Arabia.

imzad (one stringed violin) and sing during the early part of the evening. Then they go back to their tents, milk the camels and eat supper. After supper the second session of the Ahal continues far into the night as a cosy petting party. Although a man will show no sign of annoyance when a fellow Tuareg steals his girl, there is no assurance that his tolerance will extend to you.

As far as desert women are concerned, there are three factors which should hold you in check: swift, sure trouble from most tribes for violations of the code; the certainty of VD where the women are given liberty; and your sense of sight and smell.

Cleanliness among desert people varies as much as the observance of religion. If you compare a poor shepherd with an American businessman, the desert shepherd is definitely dirty. However, some wealthy Arabs wear spotlessly white garments and bathe as regularly as you do. The Moslem religion prescribes that one must wash before prayers. You will see men doing so in the entrances to mosques. The good Moslem prays five times a day. In the desert

where water is scarce he may go through the motions with sand. Religion also prescribes that both men and women must have a complete bath after sexual intercourse "even though only a small bowl of water is available." Nevertheless, many of the desert people you meet will certainly seem very dirty. Unless you have lucky contacts, you are not likely to meet many of the wealthy class who can afford the luxuries of regular baths and clean clothes.

In the deserts of Mongolia where people wipe their fingers on their garments you can smell the rancid mutton-fat almost as far as you can see the man. Even there, cleanliness varies with individuals.

Toilet habits also vary. Among most desert people their voluminous flowing robes permit them to squat and relieve themselves wherever nature calls. In oases and towns of Sahara or Arabia there are pit latrines. In some desert camps each individual will dig a small hole and cover his feces. In contrast when prickly pears are ripe in North Africa you need to watch

Photo by Dr. Wm. M. Shanklin.

An Emir of the Rwala Tribe. He is a representative in the Syrian Parliament. Note his fresh white garments. Upper class Arabs take great pride in their sparkling white headcloth and robes.

your step anywhere near a patch of that cactus. In Mongolia promiscuous defecation is practiced but the dogs consider human feces a delicacy. The final result is no worse than one finds in dog-infested residential districts of American cities.

If you are invited to eat with desert people watch their etiquette, and follow your host's lead. Among the Mongols of the Gobi, individuals carry their own food bowl and chopsticks. In Arabia and the Sahara a central dish heaped high is placed in front of the diners. Each serves himself from the section directly in front of him. You use your right hand and make an excavation in the mound of food before you. Do not encroach on the excavation of your neighbor. Each mouthful is a small "bite size" ball formed with your fingers and plopped into

your mouth. In some regions on the north edge of the Sahara spoons may be provided. If meat is served you tear it off with your right hand.

Your host may or may not appear while you are served in Arab desert regions. His women certainly will not eat until after you have been served, and you probably will not even see them. They will watch you through tiny openings in tent curtains, and will hear your conversation.

In some tribes of Arabia all diners must stop eating when one guest indicates he has finished. That means you gobble your food or leave the banquet still hungry. Among many tribes it is most courteous to belch loudly after a meal. That shows your appreciation of good cooking and bountiful food. To break wind, however, is a very serious breach of manners under any circumstances or in any Arab company.

Cooking in desert regions is all done over open fires. In Africa and Arabia you will probably find the food palatable. In some cases wood ashes will flavor the roast, sand and ashes may cling to the bread. The cooked food will be safe to eat.

You may not be enthusiastic about the tea of Mongolian deserts. Often it is thickened with flour and butter is added. Dates are good in Arabia and Africa. They vary from soft, delicious, honey delicacies to hard, dry fodder resembling peanut shucks. All are nourishing, however.

Eat the dates with your right hand and watch your companions. In some Sahara regions it is insultingly bad form to throw the date stones over your shoulder. Remove the stone from your mouth with your right hand and place it on the edge of the serving tray. Date pits are collected and crushed between rocks for camel food. Don't waste them.

When you sit in the company of desert people, sit cross-legged, tailor fashion or on your heels, depending on how the people of the region sit. Generally, it is bad form, even insulting, to show the soles of your feet when sitting in company. Your joints may creak and tire in proper position, but you will get used to it if you keep trying and live long enough.

THE RISE OF NATIONALISM

In the Sahara from Morocco to the Nile, in Arabia, in the deserts of Central Asia, and on the Gobi of Mongolia, desert people are becoming increasingly conscious of their identity as people. Like all young nations before them, they are now boasting of their independence and fanatically resent any real or fancied insult to their dignity, their customs, their religion, or their way of life.

This new spirit of nationalism makes them zealously conscious of their *Rights*. They are keenly sensitive to any form of criticism and pathetically eager for praise or recognition.

They consider it their right now to look on you as a foreigner. This is in distinct contrast to the old Colonial days when the European was able to travel as "master of all he surveyed." The radio and other improved communications have given even desert peoples a wider knowledge of the good things of the world. These include the well publicized freedoms and liberties, and the right to acquire material things formerly not only beyond their reach but beyond even their dreams.

In normal situations this simply means that you must be particularly careful to practice your natural courtesy. Be tolerant of adolescent-like boasting without trying to outboast or disillusion the man about his nationalistic or racial accomplishments. As an adult nation we can let our accomplishments speak for themselves. In short, you should act like a decent, friendly guest in a host country.

Normally if you are careful not to give offense and do not violate the religious customs and prejudices of the people, they will treat you fairly and even hospitably. During periods of political stress or national crises (like the conflict in Morocco between the French and Arab-Berber groups, and the strife in the Arab countries bordering Israel), the man in the street is apt to act as his aroused emotions dictate. When long suppressed hatreds caused by past wrongs, frustrations, or fears are suddenly released, the average man is likely to consider you or any other Westerner a fair target for his resentment.

The night in 1951 the Prime Minister of Lebanon was assassinated, I was downtown in Beiruth with another American trying to get some night photographs. We were stopped by a group of young fellows who tried to take away our camera. An educated Arab, a bit older than the members of the group, was able to talk some reason into them. We finally agreed to go to the police station together. The police wouldn't open the gates but told the group we were O.K. when I showed a leather wallet with my name in Arabic embroidered on the outside. The English-speaking Arab then escorted us a few blocks toward our quarters, and the incident was closed.

Americans or English, of course, had nothing to do with the incident which caused the roving groups to vent their emotions that night by general vandalism, breaking store windows, and preventing foreigners from taking pictures. Nevertheless we Americans were advised to keep off the streets for the next day or so.

As these notes were being collected I learned of a group of Americans who visited a remote section of Libyan Sahara in 1955. They were being hospitably escorted by a native Libyan who extended them many courtesies. Returning from the village they passed a large bundle in the road. One of the men said facetiously, "Did we get an Arab? That makes our score better for today."

Their host immediately lost his enthusiasm about entertaining the party. Where formerly he had been completely cooperative in answering questions, he now replied with only "yes" or "no." Not until the offending American left the party did the host regain his former cooperative attitude.

The group later attended a changing of the guard. In accordance with normal international courtesies they saluted the Libyan flag. That simple gesture of respect and friendship was so appreciated that the Libyans rushed out and shook hands with all the Americans. Then, at their request, repeated the ceremony so the shutterbugs could get all the photographs they wanted.

SUMMARY

Desert people have customs and forms of etiquette which are important for you to know. Since these differ from tribe to tribe, there is not enough space to give all of them in this publication. Sources in your outfit or in communities near your base will give you details for your locality.

It is important to know how to approach a desert camp and what forms are used in greeting strangers. The rules of hospitality apply to both the host and the guest. Religion is truly sacred among most desert people. It must not be ridiculed or its sacred places desecrated.

It is always safe to let women alone in deserts. They may offer you food and water if their men folks are not around. Protect your future, and *don't make passes at desert lasses.*

Desert standards of cleanliness and sanitation are not those of modern American apartment houses. "Table" manners exist among desert people, and courtesy requires that you follow them as you would expect a stranger to do in your home.

If you want to get along with strangers, get yourself a "sponsor." Among desert people if one of them, even a child, acts as your guide, the others will generally recognize his responsibility and cooperate in helping him discharge his duty to a traveler under his "safe conduct," as prescribed by the Koran.

Don't forget your manners.

Don't make facetious remarks about the people of your host country. They don't understand some brands of American humor especially when it relegates them to an inferior or ridiculous position.

Remember to extend respect and courtesies to the host peoples; both will get you more cooperation than either cash or bluster.

Don't make yourself conspicuous when desert people are emotionally wrought up by political or national crises.

Learn all you can about the people in your area before you find yourself *Afoot in the desert* and Allah-i-gauik.*

*May God strengthen you.

Appendices

Appendix 1

SIGNS AND SYMPTOMS OF DEHYDRATION IN MAN

(NOTE: This is Table 14D, p. 240, in *Physiology of Man in the Desert*, by E. F. Adolph and Associates, New York: Interscience Publishers, 1947. Items arranged in approximate order of first appearance as dehydration in the heat progresses to exhaustion and beyond.)

At deficits of body water of

1-5% of body weight	*6-10% of body weight*	*11-20% of body weight*
Thirst	Dizziness	Delirium
Vague discomfort	Headache	Spasticity
Economy of movement	Dyspnea (labored breathing)	Swollen tongue
Anorexia (no appetite)	Tingling in limbs	Inability to swallow
Flushed skin	Decreased blood volume	Deafness
Impatience	Increased blood concentration	Dim vision
Sleepiness	Absence of salivation	Shriveled skin
Increased pulse rate	Cyanosis (body blue)	Painful micturition
Increased rectal temperature	Indistinct speech	Numb skin
Nausea	Inability to walk	Anuria (defective micturition or none)

Appendix 2

LIST OF MINE HAZARDS IN LIBYA

Live mine fields from World War II ranging from 1 to 5 miles in diameter are known to exist in sections of the Libyan Desert. The following known localities were reported by 7th ARS in 1951. They probably still exist because the clearing project was halted when loss of personnel reached unreasonable numbers.

4 mile SE of Tarhuna, 32-22°N, 13-41°E.

8 mile SW of Homs, 32-45°N, 14-15°E.

3 mile NW of Sedada, 31-20°N, 14-47°E.

2 mile NW of Gheddahta, 31-32°N, 15-15°E.

2 mile SE of Bungem, 30-35°N, 15-22°E.

1 mile South of Sirte, 21-12°N, 16-24°E.

1 mile South of Mizda, 31-26°N, 12-58°E.

1 mile NW of Hun, 29-14°N, 16-00°E.

AREA 31-45°N, 14-12°E.

AREA 31-20°N, 15-18°E.

AREA 31-08°N, 14-32°E.

Other fields are uncharted. For the general areas see map—page 22.

DESERTS OF THE WORLD

Estimated Area
Square Miles

1. Afghanistan Registan .... X[20]
2. Ala Shan (part of Gobi) X
3. Arabian Desert, Arabian Peninsula 500,000
4. Arunta Desert (part of Australian Desert), Central Australia 120,000
5. Atacama, Northern Chile 70,000
6. Australian Desert, West and Central Australia X
7. Black Rock Desert, Northwestern Nevada, USA 600
8. Chilean Desert, Northwest Chile, West of Andes X
9. Chihuahua Desert—Mexico X
10. Colorado Plateau, Southeastern California, USA, part of Sonoran Desert 3,000
11. Columbian Plateau X
12. Dasht-i-Armutli, Iran East of Caspian Sea X
13. Dasht-i-Kavir, North Central Iran 18,000
14. Dasht-i-Lut, Eastern Iran 20,000
15. Dasht-i-Margo, Afghanistan X
16. Dasht-i-Naumid, Iran-Afghanistan Border.... X
17. Dxosotin Elesun, Soviet Central Asia, USSR .. X
18. Gibson Desert (part of Australian Desert), Western Australia 85,000
19. Gobi Desert, Mongolia 125,000
20. Grande Desert, Sonora, Mexico 2,500
21. Great Basin X
22. Great Barsuk, North of Aral Sea X
23. Great Salt Lake Desert, Northwestern Utah, USA 4,000
24. Great Sandy Desert (part of Australian Desert, Northwestern Australia) 160,000
25. Great Victorian Desert (part of Australian Desert, Southwestern Australia) 125,000
26. Helmand, Southern Afghanistan (both sides of Helmand River which empties into Siestan Basin) X
27. High Desert, Central Oregon, USA 3,000
28. Jafura, part of Arabian Desert, Southwest of Persian Gulf X
29. Kalahari Desert, Bechuanaland, South Africa 200,000
30. Kara-Kum, Turkmen SSR 105,000
31. Karroo, Southwest Africa (like Kalahari not true desert but very dry) X
32. Kerman Desert—South Iran X
33. Khorasan Desert (North Central Iran) same as Dasht-i-Kavir X

34. Kyzl-Kum, Uzbek SSR 90,000
35. Libyan Desert, part of Sahara 650,000
36. Madagascar Desert X
37. Mapimi Desert—Northern Mexico X
38. Mexican Plateau X
39. Mohave Desert, Southern California, USA 13,500
40. Namib Desert, South Africa X
41. Nefud (part of Arabian Desert), North and Central Saudi Arabia 50,000
42. Negev—Israel X
43. Nubian Desert (part of Sahara Desert), Northeast Anglo-Egyptian Sudan (from Red Sea to great west bend of the Nile) 100,000
44. Ordos (part of Gobi) X
45. Painted Desert, Northeastern Arizona, USA X
46. Patagonian Desert X
47. Peski Muyan-Kum, 44°N/71°E, USSR, East of Kara Tau 17,000
48. Peski Sary-Ishik-Otrau, South of Lake Balkhash, USSR X
49. Phoenix Islands. South Pacific, South of Hawaiian Islands at about 3°S and 170°W.... X
50. Priaral Desert, North of Aral Sea (see Great Barsuk Desert) X
51. Rajputana Desert, India, between Sind and Punjab X
52. Rub al Khali (part of Arabian Desert), Southeast Saudi Arabia 250,000
53. Sahara Desert 3,000,000
54. Sechura Desert, Northeastern Peru 10,000
55. Sinai Desert—East of Suez X
56. Smoke Creek Desert, Northwestern Nevada, USA 300
57. Sonoran Desert, around Gulf of California X
58. Summan Hard Desert, Part of Arabian Desert West of Persian Gulf X
59. Syrian Desert (part of Arabian Desert), Northern Arabian Peninsula 125,000
60. Takla Makan, Southern Sinkiang, China 125,000
61. Tarim Basin (contains Takla Makan) X
62. Tau Kum, part of Peski Sary—Ishik Otrau X
63. Thar Desert, Northwestern India 100,000
64. Tumbe Desert, Northern Peru X
65. Turfan Depression (part of Gobi) X
66. Vizcaino Desert, Baja California, Mexico 6,000
67. Western Argentina Desert X
68. "Western Desert," Somaliland X
69. Wyoming Basin Desert X

---

[20]X indicates that reliable estimates of area are not available.

COUNTRIES WITH ARID AND SEMIARID AREAS

Compiled by Dr. Peveril Meigs in behalf of the International
Geographical Union and revised by UNESCO Advisory
Committee on Arid Zone Research, 1951

1. *Northern Sahara Group*
    French North Africa
    Libya
    Spanish North Africa

2. *Southern Sahara-Sahel Group*
    Anglo-Egyptian Sudan
    Cameroon
    French Equatorial Africa
    French West Africa
    Nigeria

3. *East Africa Group*
    Erithrea
    Ethiopia
    Kenya
    Somaliland
    Tanganyika

4. *South Africa Group*
    Angola
    Bechuanaland
    Madagascar
    Mozambique
    South West Africa
    Southern Rhodesia
    Union of South Africa

5. *Southern Near East Group*
    Aden
    Egypt
    Iraq
    Israel
    Jordan
    Kuwait
    Lebanon
    Oman
    Saudi Arabia
    Syria
    Yemen

6. *Northern Near East Group*
    Afghanistan
    Iran
    Turkey

7. *Pakistan and India Group*
    India
    Pakistan

8. *Central Eurasia Group*
    China
    Mongolia
    U.S.S.R.

9. *Southern Europe Group*
    Greece
    Italy
    Spain

10. *Australian Group*
    Australia

11. *North America Group*
    Canada
    Mexico
    United States

12. *Brazil and Caribbean Group*
    Brazil
    Dominican Republic
    Haiti
    Puerto Rico
    Venezuela

13. *Southern and Western South America Group*
    Argentina
    Bolivia
    Chile
    Peru

14. *Isolated areas not included in major regions.*

EDIBLE DESERT PLANTS

YOU may find enough plant food in the deserts to supplement the concentrated foods of your survival kit, but don't plan on living off the native desert vegetation. It may take more energy to gather the food than you'll get by eating it.

Explorers have listed half a dozen edible plants which they have tasted while in the Gobi of Mongolia. All may be considered as agreeable supplements to your diet. They are neither plentiful enough nor substantial enough, however, to form your main food supply for many days. The list includes:

Thornbush. This is good camel food, but the young leaves can be eaten by man or steeped to make a drink like tea. The pale green inner bark is edible and has a slightly sweet taste, but a camel can eat outer bark, inner bark, and twig. You might find the twigs indigestible and the thin inner bark hardly worth the labor to separate it.

Dune-plums. These are small, berry-like drupes, each with one seed. The fruit is dark purple when ripe but may be eaten when red. The flavor resembles that of an oxheart cherry, and this fruit may be eaten raw or cooked. In some areas you can gather dune-plums by the pail full.

Rhubarb. Two kinds of rhubarb, a lowland and a highland type, are good to eat. The lowland type has a round leaf, about 1½ inches in diameter. Its two to five leaves grow close to the ground where summer rains have moistened the earth. It may be eaten raw or cooked.

The highland rhubarb is found in the Altai Mountains above 2,000 feet altitude. It has thick stalks like our garden rhubarb (pie plant) and spear-shaped leaves. You find it on broken rock and dirt on the slopes at the base of steep cliffs where moisture is available.

Onions. There are also two kinds of onions in the Gobi: hot strong little ones like scallions grow in the desert in late summer.

During this season native mutton tastes strongly of onion flavor. These will add pep to your food, but you won't want to make a meal of them. The highland onions grow 2 or 2½ inches in diameter. You can eat these like apples and can also eat the greens either raw or cooked.

Onions and other bulbs are found in other parts of the world besides the Gobi. If a bulb looks like an onion when cut in two but does not smell like an onion or like garlic *don't eat it*.

Peas. There are several kinds of peas with small seeds resembling lentils. These too may be eaten raw or cooked. Some species taste bitter unless roasted and then boiled.

Pea-like pods of plants are edible when young and tender. In mature pods the seeds and the gummy inside of the pod are both edible.

The Sahara does not have even that scanty list. In some of the dry river beds or *oueds*, a tree known as teborok (Balamites Aegyptiaca) is found. It has spiny branches and edible fruit, but no details about its taste or food value are available.

There are a few more edible plants in the deserts of southwest United States than in either the Gobi or Sahara. But you'll never get fat on them. Any of the flat leaf cactus plants like the prickly pear can be boiled and eaten as greens (like spinach) if you peel or cut off the spines first. The fruit of all cactus plants is also good to eat. Some are red and some yellow when they are ripe, but all are soft.

All cactus fruits have spines, so either cut out the spines, rub them off on the ground, or peel the fruit. The seeds of cactus fruit are small and can be eaten with the fruit. The fruit of different species varies in size from that of a cherry to that of a grapefruit.

Cacti are most abundant in the Americas but they have been introduced into Asia,

Africa, Australia and other parts of the world.

There are other plants which resemble the true cactus. The safe rule to follow is: If it looks like a cactus but has a milky juice *avoid it*.

Wild celery, wild currants, and choke cherry are all edible and are found in sections of the American desert. Indians living in that area gather pinyon nuts for food but it will try your patience to eat enough for a good meal. They are so tiny you can almost starve to death while eating them. The best advice is—don't depend on desert vegetation for your food requirements.

Sometimes after a rain there are abundant flowers in many desert regions. You can eat any flowers of the desert except possibly those with milky or colored sap.

Grasses are all edible. Usually you pull the grass blade away from the root and eat the soft tender part of the stem. All grass seeds are also edible. During the time China was occupied by Japan before World War II, many Chinese had little else but grass. One man kept a list of the different species he had eaten. Eventually he had more than 125 different species in his list.

Acacia pods are edible when young.

Succulent plants are numerous in some desert and near-desert regions. These have thick, fleshy leaves with much moisture. Some of them even look like stones so don't let their type of camouflage keep you from a juicy meal. Others are erect like the cactus. They have spines but no obvious leaves and their sap is milky. Those succulents with milky juice and those which are extremely astringent or bitter are to be avoided.

Gourds or melon—like fruit in the Sahara and Arabian deserts are generally considered poisonous although the dried seeds of old fruit have been eaten by desert survivors. The seeds are said to taste like sunflower seeds.

In the Arabian Desert there is a plant which the local people call Abal. When it is in full bloom it has red tassels and little white flowers. The flowers are edible and may be eaten raw. The dry twigs of the plant are crushed in mortars by the Bedouin to make a substitute for tea. It tastes somewhat bitter and is said to be constipating but it serves as an antidote to the salts in the waters of such desert regions as the Naifa.

Appendix 5

BIBLIOGRAPHY

1. Adolph, E. F., and Associates. *Physiology of Man in the Desert;* New York. Interscience Publishers, 1947.

2. *Air Force Manual 64-5, Survival.*

3. Alexander, Leo, Major. *The Treatment of Shock from Prolonged Exposure to Cold, Especially in Water;* Washington, D. C., Combined Intelligence Objective Subcommittee.

4. Cannon, William Austin. *Botanical Features of the Algerian Sahara;* Washington, D. C., Carnegie Institute, 1913.

5. Chalfant, W. A., *Death Valley: the Facts;* California. Stanford University Press, 1945.

6. Channing, Mark. *Indian Village.*

7. *Desert Magazine,* any spring issue, published at Palm Desert, California.

8. Feininger, Andreas. "Spring in the Desert," *Life Magazine,* 10 April 1950, pp 65-72.

9. Gautier, E. F., *Sahara the Great Desert;* New York. Columbia University Press, 1935. Translated by D. F. Mayhew.

10. Hedin, Dr. Sven. *Through Asia;* Harpers, 1898, Vols. I and II.

11. Henderson, Randall, "Bisnaga Quenched our Thirst." *Desert Magazine,* June 1950, Vol. 13, No. 8, p 20.

12. Jaeger, Edmund C., *Desert Wild Flowers;* California. Stanford University Press, 1947.

13. James, Preston E., *A Geography of Man;* Boston. Ginn and Company, 1949.

14. Philby, H. St. J. B., *Arabian Highlands;* Washington, D. C., The Middle East Institute, 1952.

15. Prejevalsky, Lt. Col. N., *Mongolia, the Tangut Country and the Solitudes of Northern Tibet;* London, 1876. Translated by E. Delmar Morgan.

16. Robins, F. W., *The Story of Water Supply;* London. Oxford University Press, 1946.

17. Schmidt-Nielsen, Bodil, and others, "Osmotic Regulation in Desert Mammals," a Memorandum Report of the USAF Air Materiel Command, Wright-Patterson Air Force Base, Ohio, 1948.

www.ingramcontent.com/pod-product-compliance
Lightning Source LLC
Chambersburg PA
CBHW080056280326
41934CB00014B/3330